FLOWER CRAFTS

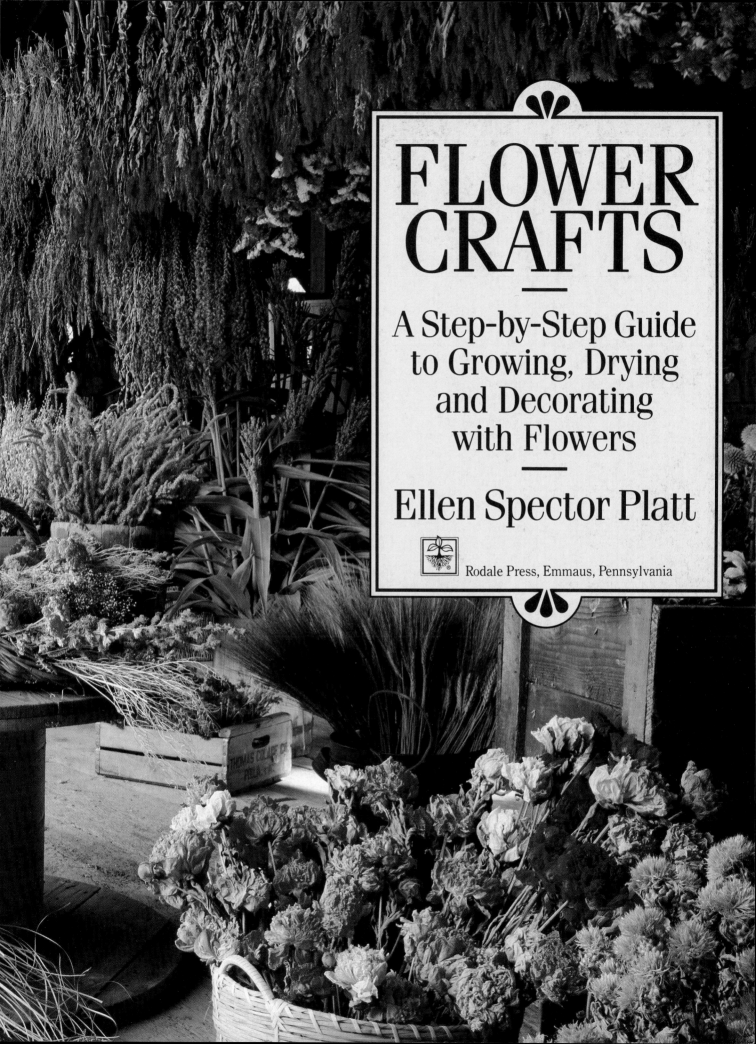

FLOWER CRAFTS

A Step-by-Step Guide
to Growing, Drying
and Decorating
with Flowers

Ellen Spector Platt

Rodale Press, Emmaus, Pennsylvania

Our Mission

We publish books that empower people's lives.

RODALE BOOKS

If you have any questions or comments concerning this book, please write:
      Rodale Press
      Book Readers' Service
      33 East Minor Street
      Emmaus, PA 18098

Library of Congress Cataloging-in-Publication Data

Platt, Ellen Spector.
      Flower crafts : a step-by-step guide to growing, drying, and decorating with flowers / by Ellen Spector Platt.
            p.   cm.
      Includes bibliographical references (p.   ) and index.
      ISBN 0-87596-148-7   hardcover
      1. Dried flower arrangement.   2. Flower garden-ing.   3. Flowers—Drying.   4. Wreaths.   5. Nature craft.   I. Title.
SB449.3.D7P58   1993
745.92—dc20   92-26611
                                                        CIP

Distributed in the book trade by St. Martin's Press

2   4   6   8   10   9   7   5   3   hardcover

Executive Editor: **Margaret Lydic Balitas**

Senior Editor: **Barbara W. Ellis**

Editor: **Nancy J. Ondra**

Project Editor: **Cheryl Winters Tetreau**

Copy Manager: **Dolores Plikaitis**

Copy Editor: **Laura Stevens**

Editorial Production Coordinator: **Susan Nickol**

Editorial/Administrative Assistant: **Karen Earl-Braymer**

Art Director: **Anita G. Patterson**

Book Designer: **Linda Jacopetti**

Cover Designers: **Linda Jacopetti and Linda Brightbill**

Photographer: **Mitch Mandel**

Photo Stylists: **Dee Schlagel, Ellen Spector Platt, and Kay Lichthardt**

Illustrator: **Frank Fretz**

Indexer: **Jean Erler**

Special thanks to the following companies for lending props used in some of the photographs:

The Antique Market Place, 2856 Lincoln Highway East, Ronks, PA 17572 (Antiques)
Curran Collection, Lynn Curran, Pottsville, PA 17901 (Antique botanical print)
Family Crafts Gift Shop, 7 East Main Street, Schuylkill Haven, PA 17972 (Americana)
Once Upon a Loom, Handwovens by Jane Lippert, R.D. 2, Box 1305, Schuylkill Haven, PA 17972 (Handwoven woolen shawls and blankets)
The Village Peddlar, Andrew Scari, U.S. Route 1, R.D. 3, Box 161B, Chadds Ford, PA 19317 (Antiques)

On the cover: Dried flowers don't have to be dull and lifeless! With a little planning and care, you can dry home-grown flowers to produce all kinds of colorful crafts. This photograph, taken at the author's barn in Orwigsburg, Pennsylvania, shows the wide range of colors available in dried flowers.

For May Spector

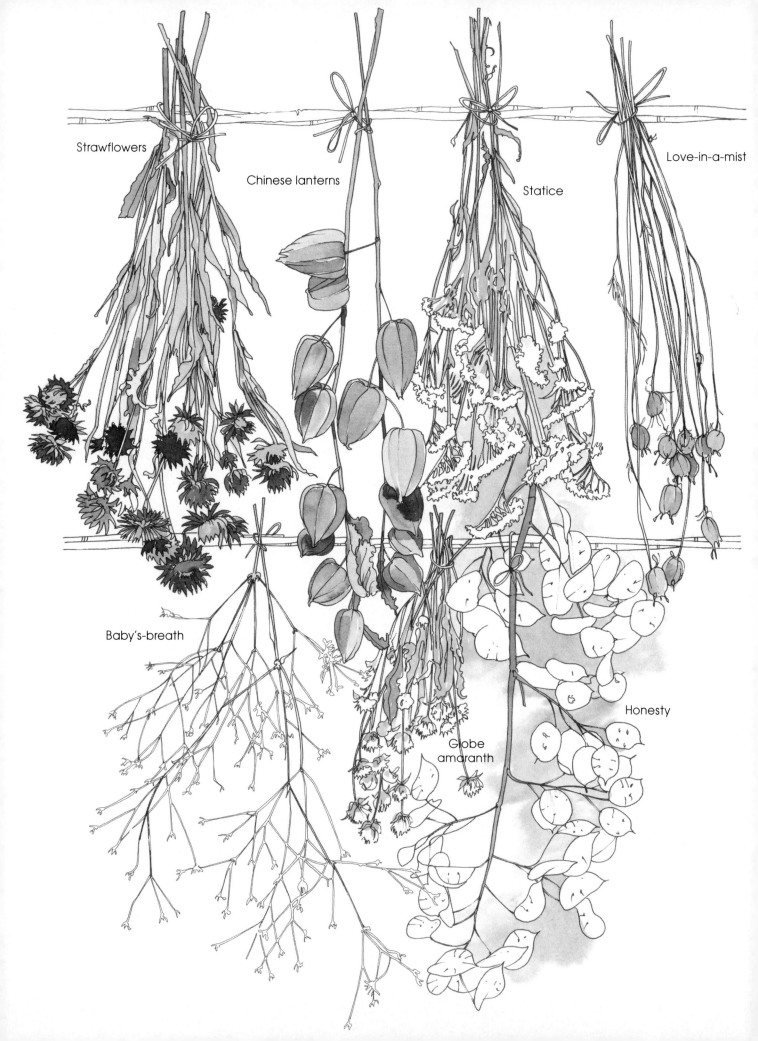

Strawflowers

Chinese lanterns

Statice

Love-in-a-mist

Baby's-breath

Globe
amaranth

Honesty

CONTENTS

INTRODUCTION

Welcome to the Meadow Lark

When people ask me, "How did you get into the flower business?" I have to answer, "By accident." Although I've had a lifelong love of flowers, I'm amazed that my childhood dream of owning a flower shop has actually come true.

In my work as a psychologist in the early 1980s, I often led workshops in career development for women. Most of the participants were women who had become full-time mothers after marriage and now hoped to enter the work force. I helped these women analyze their accomplishments and satisfactions in tasks they had performed through the years at home. Sometimes they decided to pick up the threads of their former occupations or veer off in slightly different directions. I was only vaguely aware that, through these workshops, I was teaching not only my students but also myself.

During that period, with our children in college or on their own, my husband and I moved from a modern house in town to a rundown early-nineteenth-century stone farmhouse with a large peg-and-beam barn and over five acres of land. We moved on a whim and the fantasy of restoring a once-proud structure that now stood in the way of a developer. We had no desire for horses and no particular plans for the barn. The land had been left untended for years and was an overgrown tangle. The flowering plants consisted of a solitary peony bush in the middle of the lawn and a clump of orange daylilies in another part of the lawn. Here and there a few lonely blossoms poked up: a daffodil, two hyacinths (one pink and one purple), a cluster of stars-of-Bethlehem, and a fuchsia-colored petunia which had reverted to the wild. There was a forsythia so old that its sparse blossoms seemed to disappear into the tangled brown branches. A flowering quince, two spireas, and a snowball viburnum were the only shrubs that still bloomed with confidence.

I started to rebuild the gardens even before tearing into the house restoration. Part of the land I designated as a site for wildflowers, part I planned to landscape more formally to enhance the homestead, and part my husband plowed and furrowed into neat raised beds for my first cutting garden. By the time spring arrived, I found I was spending more and more free time in the garden pulling weeds and planting. The draw to the garden felt like an addiction. The only way I could satisfy the craving was by more digging, more planting, more picking, more arranging. I started hanging bunches of flowers in the barn just to see how they would dry. I had flowers in every room of the house and gave some to friends and neighbors. The flowers kept growing, so I kept picking.

Finally, the workshops I had led claimed me as participant. I developed my long-standing interest in gardening into a part-time flower business, which I cultivated along with my psychology practice. Dried flowers seemed more compatible with my schedule than fresh, since I didn't have to sell them right away. However, there were several florists on the way to my office who were eager to have really fresh flowers. Many mornings I cut fresh flowers in the field at 6 A.M. dressed in my professional clothes plus apron and clogs. By 9 A.M. I was in my office: flowers delivered, apron whipped off, and clogs replaced by pumps. My dirty fingernails often remained as the only sign that my morning didn't start out with a leisurely breakfast and newspaper before work.

Although I had some familiarity with gardening, my only business experience was in setting up a private counseling and consulting practice. I had no training at all in floral design. Problems with drought, flooding, and garden pests and diseases seemed manageable next to the problem of marketing what I could grow. But I did have a strong educational background in research and had taught courses in research methods. It was this research bent that led me to try different methods of marketing. I talked to others with experience and made use of the strong state Cooperative Extension Service and the inexpensive educational programs and newsletters that they offer. I watched what others were doing and went to meetings, conferences, and workshops when I could find them near home. The county library had a surprisingly fine selection of books on drying flowers. Trial and plenty of error helped me to discover new flowers to dry and the proper technique for each.

While trying out different methods of marketing the flowers, I continued to add to my list of plants to grow, collect, and dry. The results of my experiments were either exciting (like when I first air dried peonies and canna leaves) or a brown mess (like when I first tried preserving bells-of-Ireland in glycerine). I started the Meadow Lark as a flower farm and added herbs and decorative vegetables in subsequent years.

One connection often led to another. When I went to the New York International Gift Show to buy baskets for my dried flowers, I stumbled upon a wholesaler who was desperate to buy unusual dried flowers. I went looking for others with the same need and found them easily, whipping out the Meadow Lark's crop list of 75 dried flowers. I scoured the newspapers and the state's list of fairs and festivals for suitable events, and through trial and error, found the ones that were most compatible with my work.

I started an open house at the Meadow Lark, and more people came each year, drawn by word of mouth, local advertising, and feature articles in several publications. The classes and workshops I offered at the Meadow Lark on dried-flower crafts were booked solid, and many students returned each year.

All these activities, of course, took time, and I cut down the hours in my office, then stopped my consulting activities. Averse to taking risks, I made the cuts gradually until I could see some income from the farm. At first the garden was simply a part of my personal stress-management program, then it became an exciting new part-time business. But the pull of farming finally seduced me to close my practice in 1990 to spend all my working hours at the Meadow Lark.

This book is a result of all of the things I've learned as a grower and arranger of dried and fresh flowers at Meadow Lark Flower and Herb Farm. I've included complete instructions for a wide range of seasonal projects as well as tips on growing and drying your own flowers (chapters 1 and 2) and choosing and using craft materials (page 147). I hope that reading this book will help inspire you to enjoy the pleasure of growing, crafting, and decorating with flowers.

Special Thanks

I have received help in the garden from many wonderful people who allowed themselves to be dragooned into hot, dirty work and others who helped me with the harder work of selling my produce. Each lent his or her talents in unique ways: Toni Groff, Emily Leinheiser, Jewel Robinson, Dave Platt, Linda Clinton, Mike Platt, Emily West Platt, Don and Ryan Pentz, Jenny Hopkins, Mark Hopkins, Alena and Sarah Hopkins, Rob Wexler, Saretta and Dan Berlin, and Nicola Karras.

My advisors Leila Kern, Esq., Adele M. Brodkin, Joan Steel, and Barbara Pressler contributed their invaluable professional expertise. Benjamin B. Platt showed me the error of my ways and led me to computer heaven. He continues to make emergency house calls whenever my Mac balks.

The creative team at Rodale Press has been a joy to work with—always stimulating, challenging, knowledgeable, and above all, helpful. Special "thank yous" to my editor, Nancy J. Ondra, whose knowledge of gardening continues to astound me; to the talented photographer Mitch Mandel for his elegant interpretation of my work (and for his appreciation of my cooking); to Linda Jacopetti for her outstanding book design and her enthusiasm; to senior editor Barbara W. Ellis for her help, support, and photographic skills; to Troy Schneider for his unique eye; to Frank Fretz for his ability to turn even a spool of wire into a small gem; and to executive editor Margaret Lydic Balitas who bought my first pressed flowers and who started my career as a garden crafts writer.

Ellen Spector Platt

Ellen Spector Platt

Experience the pleasure of crafting with home-grown and dried flowers. Here are just a few of the projects you can make with flowers and plants from your garden (clockwise, from top): Rose Ring (page 56), Dried Topiary Tree (page 90), Peony Pocket (page 56), Plate Ring (page 78), and Dried Flowers in a French Style (page 72).

FROM SEED TO POD: THE DRYER'S GARDEN

You have a treat in store if you haven't yet tried growing flowers to dry. More than likely you already have at least one plant in your garden that would dry well. Besides the well-known annual everlastings, such as statice and strawflowers, many perennials and bulbs produce flowers that are easy to dry. As your interest in crafting with flowers grows, you may want to add a few new plants to your garden each year. Or if you already know what plants you want and you have the room to grow them, you could plant them all at one time and have a wealth of craft material for years to come. In this chapter, I'll describe some of the advantages of growing your own craft flowers, and the simple techniques I use to have a productive garden without expensive equipment.

Why Grow Your Own?

Perhaps the best reason to grow your own craft flowers is the satisfaction you get from nurturing a tiny plant and helping it to grow strong and healthy. When you use flowers that you've grown for crafts, your projects become even more of a personal creation. I must admit that I get a secret thrill when I come across some of my flowers in an office or a home, handsome and well arranged. The feeling is not unlike that of seeing my children perform well at some public event.

Growing your own flowers has tangible benefits as well—you'll get the best-looking flowers at the best price. If you have to rely on store-bought flowers, you are often faced with a limited supply and variety. Those you do find may have faded colors or be poorly formed because they were picked at the wrong time. Growers often strip off all the leaves to speed the drying process, leaving the flowers with long, naked stems.

As these commercially grown flowers are packed in boxes and shipped for long distances, it's inevitable that some of the flowers will get crushed or at least misshapen in transit. The flowers that make it to the store in one piece are usually snatched up right away, so you are left to choose from the less desirable flowers unless you're there when a new shipment comes in. Fortunately,

growing your own flowers can help you avoid all of these problems, so you can create the most beautiful crafts with the finest floral materials.

Top Quality

One of the advantages of growing your own craft flowers is that you get the best quality available. When you grow the flowers yourself, you can harvest them at their peak and dry them promptly so they'll retain their bright colors. You are also free to experiment with picking plants at different stages to get just the colors and shapes that you need. Since you'll be working with relatively small quantities of flowers, you can dry them individually or in small bunches, eliminating the need to strip away the green beauty of the leaves. When you are ready to arrange the flowers, you'll have the pleasure of working with sturdy, well-shaped blossoms.

Unlimited Variety

Growing your own flowers also gives you the widest range of plant forms and colors to choose from. While strawflowers and statice are fairly easy to find in craft stores, you probably won't see dried peonies or lilies on the shelves. Plants like baptisias, bachelor's-buttons, and bells-of-Ireland are seldom offered for sale in the retail market as dried flowers but are still wonderful for craft work. Your garden can provide you with all of these materials and more.

Part of the fun of drying is experimenting with flowers that other people don't normally try to dry. Some of my most exciting successes have been with drying "unusual" plants, such as dogwood and wisteria. Any plant with an interesting flower, leaf, or pod is fair game for drying! These unusual materials can add extra interest to even the simplest craft.

Designing a Garden for Crafts

Whether your yard is large or small, you can grow a wide range of plants for craft materials. But even before you decide what plants to grow, you need to figure out where you're going to put them. If you aren't planning to cut much for craft work, you may just want to add new plants to your existing landscape. But if you plan to grow lots of different plants for craft work, you might decide to group all of those plants together in a separate cutting garden.

The Integrated Landscape

Even if you don't have room for the luxury of a separate cutting garden, you can still experience the fun of growing plants for crafts. Simply interplant trees, shrubs, and flowers for drying throughout your garden as part of your overall landscape plan. Large pussy willow and hydrangea bushes, for example, are useful background plants. Red twig dogwood stems viewed from indoors brighten a dull winter day. Roses, scotch brooms, and small contorted hazelnut trees are easy to incorporate into a mixed border.

A perennial bed or border can also provide material for crafting. You can sneak a few stems of peony, globe thistle, or yarrow from the perennial bed to dry without missing them too much. If it doesn't break your heart, you can even harvest some exquisite delphiniums in the prime of their life from the back of the border, to air dry for a winter arrangement. Annual everlastings are also attractive companions for perennials or bedding plants. You can mix them into beds and borders to add spots of bright color, and snip a few blooms as you need them for your projects.

In many cases, though, cutting a quantity of plant material can leave unsightly gaps in your garden. It can be hard to go out and cut all of the flowers you want without feeling guilty about spoiling the floral display. But if you don't need to cut too much, incorporating your craft plants into the landscape allows you to enjoy their beauty both indoors in crafts and outside in the garden.

The Cutting Garden

With my first cutting garden, my life changed. No more did I timidly pluck one or two stems from the back of a plant, trying to prevent a de-

Create a cutting garden. *A cutting garden can be a useful and colorful addition to your landscape. You'll always have plenty of flowers to pick, and you can enjoy their beauty in the garden as well as in your crafts.*

nuded look; no more was there a "should I or shouldn't I?" conflict when I wanted to dry an armload of flowers. It was the feeling of abandon and abundance in the cutting garden that led me toward my own flower business.

While the main purpose of a cutting garden is to pick all the flowers as soon as they're ready, it can still be attractive for most of the year. You don't have to hide it away behind some barrier. I have designed three separate cutting-garden layouts, the first two primarily with flowers for air drying and the third with flowers excellent for pressing. Although the theme of these gardens is drying, all of the flowers are wonderful fresh-cut as well. Use one of these plans in its entirety or as a basis for designing your own plan. Flowers that air dry well also generally press well–the reverse, however, is not always true. Feel free to transpose plants from one garden to the other.

Starting from Seed

If you want interesting, high-quality flowers in your crafts, you'll need to grow and dry them yourself. However, buying plants (especially perennials) in quantity becomes an expensive proposition. After many years of doing just that, I was astonished to discover that many perennials are as easy to start from seed as zinnias. Yarrows, globe thistles (*Echinops* spp.), baby's-breaths, globe centaureas (*Centaurea macrocephala*), gay-feathers (*Liatris* spp.), gloriosa daisies (*Rudbeckia hirta* 'Gloriosa Daisy'), and delphiniums are a few that bloom the first year from seed started indoors with no special treatment.

Annuals, of course, are quite easy to start from seed. Growing your own gives you a wide selection of plant sizes and colors to choose from, all for the price of a packet of seed. Besides being more expensive, the bedding plants that you'll find at your local garden center are commonly limited to a few cultivars, not all of which are suitable for drying. For example, plants of the common 6- to 8-inch, mound-forming ageratum are readily available wherever annuals are sold, but their stems are too short to work with in arrangements. To get a 20- to 30-inch ageratum that is excellent both for cutting and drying (such as 'Blue Horizon'), you'll have to start it yourself. Annual seeds are often sold by individual colors as well as in mixes, so you don't have to grow a whole range of colors if you really just want one or two.

Deciding What to Grow

Perhaps the hardest part of starting plants from seed is deciding what to grow. To help narrow the choices, ask yourself what you really want for your garden. Do you want to concentrate on dependable, easy-to-grow perennials such as baby's-breath, German statice, and yarrow? Or are you willing to experiment with more unusual plants, like unicorn plant or cotton? (If you have limited space, you might want to concentrate on growing the uncommon flowers that you can't get at the store.) Do you want to stick with one color theme, such as blues and purples, or would you prefer a wide range of colors?

Also think about what crafts you like to do. If you like to create arrangements, you'll need a range of flower forms, including spiky flowers (like delphiniums), rounded flowers (like globe thistles), and airy fillers (like baby's-breaths). If you enjoy pressed flowers, make sure your garden has lots of smaller flowers. Leaves can also add some much-needed green to your dried-flower projects. And remember to add a few new plants that you can experiment with in your garden and your crafts.

Once you know roughly what kinds of plants you are looking for, there are a few other points to keep in mind. When you are looking for plants for drying, check the plant height. In general, it's best to choose the taller cultivars; you'll find that it's easier to shorten a stem than it is to lengthen it. There are, for instance, some large-headed but short-stemmed celosia that are inconvenient to use in arrangements without extending the stems with wire or floral picks.

When you choose the flower color, keep in mind that colors tone down no matter how carefully you dry the flowers. Because the colors become muted, it is usually better to start with vibrant colors rather than pastels. After drying, a brilliant (some say garish) red salvia like 'Firecracker' or 'Pirate' becomes a lovely muted version of its former self; the salmon and pink salvias become too dull. True everlastings like straw-flowers and globe amaranth, however, are valuable as pastels, since they can last years without noticeable fading.

Once you decide what to grow, the next step is learning where to find the seeds. Don't limit yourself to the seeds available at local garden centers–they often only stock the most popular flowers in a limited range of colors. For the best

(continued on page 10)

GOLDEN GLOW GARDEN

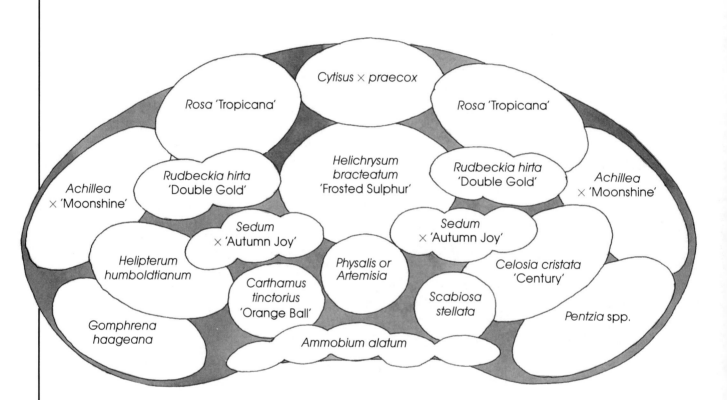

This mixture of annuals, perennials, and shrubs will brighten your garden as well as your crafts. Choose either 'Silver King' artemisia or Chinese lanterns for the tub in the center of the garden. Sitting on the surface, or buried in the garden almost up to its rim, the tub will keep either of these invasive plants from taking over your garden. All of these plants are easy to air dry, and they thrive on a site with full sun and average, well-drained soil. The numbers of plants or seed packets given on the opposite page will fill a 15 × 7½-foot area.

Name	Color When Dried	Height	Quantity
Achillea × 'Moonshine' ('Moonshine' yarrow)	Old gold flowers	3–4 feet	2 plants
Ammobium alatum (winged everlasting)	White flowers with dark gold centers	1½ feet	1 packet
Artemisia ludoviciana 'Silver King' ('Silver King' artemisia)	Silver gray leaves	2 feet	3 plants
Carthamus tinctorius 'Orange Ball' ('Orange Ball' safflower)	Orange flowers with green calyxes (bases)	1½ feet	1 packet
Celosia cristata 'Century' ('Century' plumed celosia)	Scarlet, rusty red, or honey-colored flowers	1½ feet	1 packet
Cytisus × *praecox* (Scotch broom)	Green stems	4 feet	1 plant
Gomphrena haageana (Orange globe amaranth)	Orange flowers	1½ feet	1 packet
Helichrysum bracteatum 'Frosted Sulphur' ('Frosted Sulphur' strawflower)	Pale yellow flowers	3 feet	1 packet
Helipterum humboldtianum	Vivid gold flowers	1½ feet	1 packet
Pentzia spp. (pentzias)	Yellow and gold flowers	1 foot	1 packet
Physalis alkekengi (Chinese lantern)	Orange pods	1½ feet	3 plants
Rosa 'Tropicana' ('Tropicana' rose)	Bright coral flowers	4 feet	2 plants
Rudbeckia hirta 'Double Gold' ('Double Gold' gloriosa daisy)	Gold flowers with brown centers	3 feet	4 plants
Scabiosa stellata	Tan seed heads	2 feet	1 packet
Sedum × 'Autumn Joy' ('Autumn Joy' sedum)	Chocolate brown seed heads	2 feet	6 plants

PINK AND BLUE GARDEN

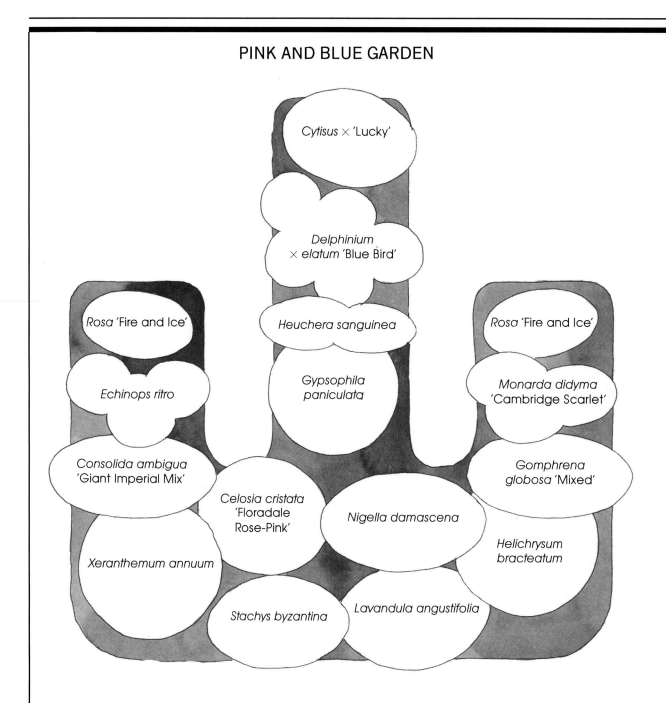

Cytisus × 'Lucky'

Delphinium × elatum 'Blue Bird'

Rosa 'Fire and Ice'

Heuchera sanguinea

Rosa 'Fire and Ice'

Echinops ritro

Gypsophila paniculata

Monarda didyma 'Cambridge Scarlet'

Consolida ambigua 'Giant Imperial Mix'

Gomphrena globosa 'Mixed'

Celosia cristata 'Floradale Rose-Pink'

Nigella damascena

Xeranthemum annuum

Helichrysum bracteatum

Stachys byzantina

Lavandula angustifolia

If you enjoy growing flowers for both fresh and dried use, try this garden. It contains primarily pink- and blue-flowered plants, along with some silver and white for a pleasant contrast. The design also features short paths, which make it easy to reach the flowers for cutting and allow for good air circulation among the plants. All of these plants air dry well and will thrive in full sun and average, well-drained soil (although the delphiniums appreciate a little extra fertilizer and moisture). Using the numbers of plants suggested on the opposite page, this design fits in a 12 × 12-foot area.

Name	Color When Dried	Height	Quantity
Celosia cristata 'Floradale Rose-Pink' ('Floradale Rose-Pink' cockscomb)	Bright pink flowers	20 inches	1 packet
Consolida ambigua 'Giant Imperial Mix' ('Giant Imperial Mix' larkspur)	White, blue, pink, or purple flowers	4 feet	1 packet
Cytisus × 'Lucky' ('Lucky' Scotch broom)	Green stems	4 feet	1 plant
Delphinium × *elatum* 'Blue Bird' ('Blue Bird' delphinium)	True blue flowers	5 feet	5 plants
Echinops ritro (globe thistle)	Steel blue flower heads	4 feet	3 plants
Gomphrena globosa 'Mixed' ('Mixed' globe amaranth)	White, pink, lavender, or purple flowers	15 inches	1 packet
Gypsophila paniculata (baby's-breath)	White flowers	3 feet	1 plant
Helichrysum bracteatum 'Bikini Pink' ('Bikini Pink' strawflowers)	Pink flowers	1 foot	1 packet
Heuchera sanguinea (coral bells)	Bright pink flowers	15 inches	2 plants
Lavandula angustifolia (lavender)	Lavender-blue flowers	2 feet	3 plants
Monarda didyma 'Cambridge Scarlet' ('Cambridge Scarlet' bee balm)	Deep-pink flowers	3 feet	3 plants
Nigella damascena (love-in-a-mist)	Green pods with maroon stripes	15 inches	1 packet
Rosa 'Fire and Ice' ('Fire and Ice' rose)	Wine-red flowers with white highlights	4 feet	2 plants
Stachys byzantina (lamb's-ears)	Silver gray leaves	2 feet	2 plants
Xeranthemum annuum (immortelle)	White, pink, or lavender flowers	15 inches	1 packet

PERFECT-FOR-PRESSING GARDEN

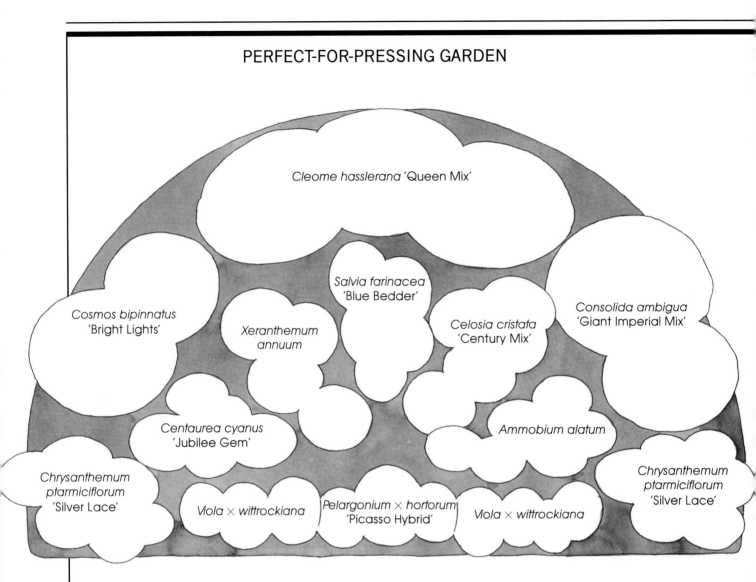

Cleome hasslerana 'Queen Mix'

Salvia farinacea 'Blue Bedder'

Cosmos bipinnatus 'Bright Lights'

Xeranthemum annuum

Celosia cristata 'Century Mix'

Consolida ambigua 'Giant Imperial Mix'

Centaurea cyanus 'Jubilee Gem'

Ammobium alatum

Chrysanthemum ptarmiciflorum 'Silver Lace'

Viola × wittrockiana

Pelargonium × hortorum 'Picasso Hybrid'

Viola × wittrockiana

Chrysanthemum ptarmiciflorum 'Silver Lace'

With this garden, you'll never be at a loss for materials to use in pressed flower crafts. If you grow your own annuals from seed, choose seeds in mixed colors to get the best range of floral material for crafts. And don't forget to pick leaves for pressing, too—geraniums, sages, larkspurs, and cosmos all produce attractive, easy-to-press leaves. All of these plants are annuals or tender perennials grown as annuals; all but the front row will self-sow for next year. These plants thrive in full sun and average, well-drained soil. With the number of plants or seed packets suggested on the opposite page, this garden will fill a 15 × 7½-foot space.

Name	Color When Dried	Height	Quantity
Ammobium alatum (winged everlasting)	White flowers with dark gold centers	1½ feet	1 packet
Celosia cristata 'Century Mix' ('Century Mix' plumed celosia)	Pink, red, or yellow flowers	8 inches	1 packet
Centaurea cyanus 'Jubilee Gem' ('Jubilee Gem' bachelor's-button)	True blue flowers	14 inches	1 packet
Chrysanthemum ptarmiciflorum 'Silver Lace' ('Silver Lace' dusty miller)	Gray leaves	7 inches	12 plants
Cleome hasslerana 'Queen Mix' ('Queen Mix' spider flower)	White, pink, rose, or purple flowers	5 feet	1 packet
Consolida ambigua 'Giant Imperial Mix' ('Giant Imperial Mix' larkspur)	White, blue, pink, or purple flowers	4 feet	1 packet
Cosmos bipinnatus 'Bright Lights' ('Bright Lights' cosmos)	Yellow, orange, and scarlet flowers	3 feet	1 packet
Pelargonium × *hortorum* 'Picasso Hybrid' ('Picasso Hybrid' zonal geranium)	Deep-red flowers	14 inches	10 plants
Salvia farinacea 'Blue Bedder' ('Blue Bedder' sage)	Lavender-blue flowers	22 inches	3 plants
Viola × *wittrockiana* (pansy)	White, blue, red, or yellow flowers	8 inches	12 plants
Xeranthemum annuum (immortelle)	White, pink, or lavender flowers	15 inches	1 packet

selection, mail order is the way to go. But don't look at just one or two catalogs: Different companies offer different cultivars and colors. One may specialize in selling separate colors of popular annuals, such as globe amaranth and strawflower, while another only offers mixed seeds. Looking through several catalogs will give you a good idea of the plants and colors that are available. See Appendix D on page 154 for a listing of some excellent seed catalogs.

When you've gotten the seeds that you want to grow, then you need to decide how and where you want to plant them. "Starting Seeds Indoors" (below) tells you how to get an early start on spring by growing your seeds in pots or seed trays in the house. "Direct Sowing" on page 13 explains how to plant seeds outdoors where you want them to grow.

Starting Seeds Indoors

Starting seedlings indoors gives you a jump on the growing season, and thus a higher yield from annuals that can be harvested throughout the summer. For instance, I start picking straw-flowers in July from my transplanted seedlings, while the direct-sown seeds of the same cultivar in the next row may not bloom for at least another month. In short-season areas, you may have to plant out seedlings in order to get any flowers at all before frost.

Indoor starting is a necessity for some plants in some parts of the country. Long-season crops, like ornamental cotton, may need the extra growing time indoors to mature before fall frosts. Some perennials, like yarrow, will bloom the first year if you start them early enough indoors. "Seeds to Start Indoors" on the opposite page gives you a list of many plants that are best to start indoors in most areas.

Choosing a Container

There are many acceptable containers and methods for starting seeds indoors. I prefer to use plastic trays (also known as flats) with liners divided into 48 or 72 compartments per tray. The 48-cell liners are best for plants started early in the season, like delphiniums and other perennials; the larger cells allow plenty of room for the roots to develop until the seedlings are transplanted outdoors. You can also use plastic pots or home-made containers for starting seeds indoors.

I fill my containers with a commercially blended seed-starting mix. This medium is loose,

so the tender roots can penetrate it easily, but it holds a good amount of moisture. It has also been sterilized, which helps prevent the fungal diseases that can attack seedlings. If you don't want to buy a mix just for seedlings, you can make your own by combining equal parts of peat moss and perlite or vermiculite. (You can buy all of these products at your local garden center.) Don't use garden soil for starting seeds indoors. It packs down, inhibiting root growth, and it contains weed seeds and diseases that can compete with or kill your seedlings.

Before you fill the containers, moisten the seed-starting mix. The easiest way to do this is to pour it into a large bowl or bucket and add warm water until the mix is evenly moist. If the water doesn't soak in right away, it helps to knead the mix with your hands. Or if you're not in a hurry, let the water soak into the mix overnight. Keep in mind that it's usually better to add too little water than too much. The mix should feel moist but should not drip when you squeeze it lightly. If the mix is still too dry, add more water. If it is too wet, add more dry mix and work it in until you get the mix evenly moist.

Providing Enough Light

At the Meadow Lark, I don't have the luxury of a greenhouse or plant growth lights. My indoor growing space is limited to windowsills and is therefore precious. I start by sorting my seeds into three piles: Those that prefer to be directly sown, those that need to be started indoors, and those that can be handled either way. The seeds in the "indoors" pile get top priority for window-sill space. If there is any room left over, I'll sow seeds from the "either way" pile as well.

I rely on seed package directions, growing charts in seed catalogs, and seed-starting pamphlets, which many companies offer, for information on the sowing requirements of each species. One major distinction is whether seeds need light or dark to germinate. If the seeds need light, as strawflowers do, plant them on the surface of the growing medium and carefully press them down. Plant most other kinds of seeds so they are covered with growing medium, usually to the same thickness of the seed. If you know the seeds need darkness to germinate, as pansies do, cover the sown flats with newspapers or cardboard to exclude all light. Check under the cover daily, and remove it as soon as you see the seedlings emerge from the soil.

Starting seeds indoors. *You don't need a greenhouse to grow your own bedding plants—all they need is a bright windowsill. Turning the trays every day helps keep the stems straight.*

spots for trays of snapdragons, delphiniums, and pearly everlasting (*Anaphalis margaritacea*), which prefer cool temperatures. Warm, sunny rooms, such as those on the south side of the house, are ideal for heat-loving plants like blue sage (*Salvia farinacea*), dahlias, and purple coneflowers (*Echinacea* spp.). Other, less fussy flowers like zinnias and marigolds can be put wherever there is room and told they will just have to make do.

Keeping the Humidity High

Once you find a place for the sown flats, cover them with plastic wrap to provide extra humidity until germination. When the tiny sprouts are visible, remove the plastic covering. Otherwise, the plants will have soft, succulent stems that are prone to disease. Keep the medium slightly moist, but not wet, at all times. Water from the bottom so small seeds won't get dislodged or washed away; for complete instructions, see the illustration on page 12.

Overwatering can damage the fragile seedlings and make them prone to fungal diseases. If your seedlings wilt suddenly right at the base (a problem called damping-off) or if a grayish white film starts to grow on the surface of the medium, reduce watering to limit the spread of the problem. It is much easier, though, to avoid such problems than it is to cure them, so be sure to water the seedlings only when the top ¼ to ½ inch of soil is dry. Good air circulation also helps keep seedlings sturdy and healthy.

Caring for Seedlings

If your seedlings are totally dependent on natural light, as mine are, you'll often find that

Providing the Right Temperature

Seed packets also usually list preferred germination temperatures. Sometimes it can be difficult to provide all the different ideal temperatures. However, there are micro-climates inside your house, and it's worth your time to scout them out. The north side of the house usually has the shadiest and coolest rooms; these can be good

SEEDS TO START INDOORS

Because my indoor growing space is limited, I only sow the ones that really benefit from a head start. Here's a list of the seeds—both perennials and annuals—that I usually start indoors.

Achillea spp. (yarrows)
Ageratum houstonianum (ageratum)
Anaphalis margaritacea (pearly everlasting)
Antirrhinum majus (snapdragon)
Belamcanda chinensis (blackberry lily)
Celosia cristata (cockscomb)

Craspedia globosa (craspedia)
Delphinium spp. (delphiniums)
Gossypium hirsutum (cotton)
Lavandula angustifolia (lavender)
Viola × *wittrockiana* (pansy)

the stems get long and spindly after a few cloudy days. And even when the spring is sunny, the seedlings that are farthest from the window may bend toward the light. Every morning the first chore of the day is rotating all the trays of seedlings in an effort to keep the stems straight. Don't worry if your seedlings don't look as good as the ones sold at the garden center; yours will straighten up once they are transplanted into the garden.

As the seedlings continue to grow, thin out any crowded compartments to one seedling per cell. Use scissors to cut off unwanted seedlings at the soil level; pulling them out may damage the roots of the seedling you want to save. Some plants benefit from a light pinching to make them bushier with side growth. Plants with upright stems, including bee balms, mints, sages, and zinnias, will produce sideshoots if you pinch back the growing tip. Pinching won't help clump-forming plants, like coneflowers, poppies, statice, and yarrows. Wait until the seedlings are a few inches tall and have several sets of true leaves before you decide whether or not to pinch them. Use your fingernails or a sharp pair of scissors to break off the stem tip cleanly, leaving at least two pairs of leaves on the remaining stem. Don't pull on the seedlings as you remove the tops, or you may damage the stems or roots in the process.

Don't worry about fertilizing until the seedlings have at least two sets of true leaves. After that, I add fish emulsion, mixed at one-quarter of the strength recommended on the label, every other time I water. Keep in mind that too much fertilizer can damage your plants as easily as too much water. If you forget to add fertilizer for a week or two, don't apply twice as much to the plants when you do remember—if you do, you may wind up with a whole crop of damaged or dead plants.

Hardening-Off Seedlings

About a week before planting time, you can start to "harden-off" the flats of seedlings. Until now, your seedlings were used to warm indoor temperatures and indirect light. Gradually exposing the plants to the direct sun and cooler temperatures will help them adapt better once you plant them in the garden.

Because I have so many seedlings, I prefer to move them all outdoors at once. They sit in rows on my sheltered, south-facing front porch, snuggled against the stone house for protection from the north winds. If there's danger of frost at night,

Bottom watering of seedlings. To encourage a deep root system on your seedlings, always water them from below. Pour about ½ inch of water into the tray they are sitting in, and let them soak up the moisture they need.

I drape large sheets of plastic over the flats to protect them from the cooler evening temperatures, and remove the sheets in the morning. If you are willing to take the time, it's often better to move the flats outdoors during the day to a partly shady place and bring them back in for the first few nights. After that, you can gradually expose the seedlings to more sun and nighttime temperatures. The plants will dry out more quickly outdoors than they did inside, so check them every day and water when necessary. After about a week, your seedlings should be ready for the garden.

Transplanting

Whether you grow your own or buy them, small seedlings need extra care when you set them out in the garden. Before you start transplanting, of course, you'll need to prepare the planting site—for complete details, see "Preparing the Soil" on page 14. When you are ready to transplant, dampen the growing medium before you remove the seedlings from the flat. Also

How to hold a seedling for transplanting.
Always hold a young seedling by the tip of its leaf when transplanting, to avoid damaging its tender stem. Use your other hand to make a hole in the soil.

water as the seedlings recover from the transplant shock.

Garden books always recommend transplanting late in the afternoon or on a cloudy day to lessen the shock of the sunshine on the seedlings. While this advice is excellent, what can you do if the only day you can plant turns out to be warm and sunny? Transplant anyway, as I do. Try to water more often to help the plants recover from the radical treatment. You could also try shading the seedlings with newspaper for a few hours, until the sun goes down.

I usually start transplanting some of my hardened-off seedlings about a week after the frost date, always beginning with the most cold-tolerant ones. The calendulas are the first to go in; the snapdragons, delphiniums, and monks-hoods (*Aconitum* spp.) soon follow. If I'm unlucky and there is a late frost, I have no recourse. My garden is too big, and there is just too much area to run out and cover the seedlings once they are planted in the field. In a smaller garden, you can protect individual plants with cloches, or drape small beds with plastic sheets, old shower curtains, or whatever lightweight material you have. Be sure to prop up the covers with short stakes to keep them from crushing the fragile seedlings. For more ideas on seedling protection, see the illustration on page 15.

Direct Sowing

In many cases, I prefer to sow seeds directly in the garden. It's easier and cheaper this way: no buying seed trays, starting medium, or plastic wrap; no turning trays to catch the light; no watching for the dreaded damping-off fungus; no hardening-off; and no rushing out to cover transplants. Indoor space is so limited, I would rather reserve it for top-priority plants. "Seeds to Direct-Sow" on page 14 lists several seeds that require or tolerate planting right into the garden.

When deciding which seeds to start outdoors, remember that the bigger the seed, the more chance of success in the garden. Large seeds, like those from safflowers (*Carthamus tinctorius*) and sunflowers, are easy to space in rows and will rarely wash away. Plants that develop deep taproots, such as poppies and lupines, don't enjoy being transplanted, so plant them where you want them to grow.

Direct sowing is the best treatment for several kinds of annuals. With flowers like love-in-a-mist that don't rebloom and give only one crop a

moisten the soil where you are going to plant them, and make a hole large enough to receive the roots. Plant the seedlings at the same depth as they were growing in the pot or flat. If I am transplanting seedlings with spindly stems, I often make the hole a bit deeper so I can bury the stem up to the first set of leaves.

With individual cell packs, push up the bottom of the plastic to loosen the mass of roots and growing medium, and gently slide the plant out. If you planted all the seeds together in one tray, carefully lift out each seedling with the tip of a pencil. Avoid touching the roots or the weak stem. Holding each seedling by the leaves, move it to the prepared hole, and gently tamp the soil around the roots. Water well after transplanting. Expect some drooping that day or next, but continue to summer, there is no advantage to the longer growing season that you could provide by using transplants. You can even sow hardy annuals, like larkspur and love-in-a-mist, directly in the garden the previous September. This method gives an early spring crop in the cool weather these plants prefer.

Once the planting site is ready (see "Preparing the Soil" below), the actual planting is a very quick job. Large seeds, which generally produce larger plants, are ideal for planting in rows. The rows will keep the plants evenly spaced, so they'll each have enough room to grow to their full size. To help keep your rows straight, scratch lines into the planting area with a stick or the end of a tool handle.

When starting smaller seeds directly in the garden, it is harder to control the placement of the seeds than when you start them indoors in flats. You might think that a seed packet containing a hundred seeds will produce a lot of plants, but those tiny seeds can be gone in three pinches of your fingers, leaving you with the rest of the flower bed to fill. If you have small seeds to sow, take a coffee can and put in about a cup of dry white play sand (not seashore sand, which contains salt that can damage seedlings). Pour the seeds directly from the package into the sand, and stir. Now when you sow the seed-sand mixture in a row or broadcast it over a bed, you will be sowing the seeds more evenly and spreading them a little farther. You'll also have less thinning to do, thus wasting fewer precious seeds.

Check seed packages for the recommended sowing depth. A common mistake is to plant the seeds too deeply, so they run out of energy before they can break through the soil. If you can't find a depth reference for your seeds, a good general rule is to cover them no deeper than the thickness of the seed: usually $1/16$ to $1/8$ inch deep. Rake the bed lightly to cover the seeds with soil, and then use the bottom of the rake to tamp down the sown bed. Some seeds, like those of strawflowers and bells-of-Ireland, need light to germinate; press these seeds into the soil, but don't cover them.

If you can, water gently right after sowing and every day thereafter until the seeds germinate and the tiny plants appear. I say "if you can" because there will undoubtedly be some days that time runs out before your gardening chores get done. Fortunately, as with most aspects of gardening, you have some leeway. Seeds are "programmed" to germinate and often will do so despite benign neglect. In general, though, the few extra minutes you take to care for the seedlings will reward you with ample blossoms later in the summer.

Preparing the Soil

The simplest way to prepare soil is to pull out or till under all weeds and undesirable vegetation. Then loosen the top 6 to 12 inches of soil with a spade, spading fork, or tiller. Add compost or any other soil amendment that you plan to use, and work it into the loosened soil with the same tools. Rake the area smooth, and you are ready to plant.

Sounds pretty simple, doesn't it? Well, it is. I admire scientific gardeners who regularly test their soil and who pay great attention to the exact nutrient needs of their plants. No doubt they get better results than I do—but I can testify that "lazy," unscientific methods also work.

At the Meadow Lark, I have several areas for

SEEDS TO DIRECT-SOW

Many plants grow easily from seed planted directly in the garden. Here's a list of some of the easiest annuals and perennials to start this way.

Ammobium alatum (winged everlasting)
Carthamus tinctorius (safflower)
Centaurea cyanus (bachelor's-button)
Cleome hasslerana (spider flower)
Consolida ambigua (rocket larkspur)
Cosmos bipinnatus (cosmos)
Helipterum spp. (helipterums)

Lunaria annua (honesty)
Lupinus spp. (lupines)
Nigella damascena (love-in-a-mist)
Papaver orientale (Oriental poppy)
Salvia splendens (scarlet sage)
Xeranthemum annuum (immortelle)
Zinnia elegans (zinnia)

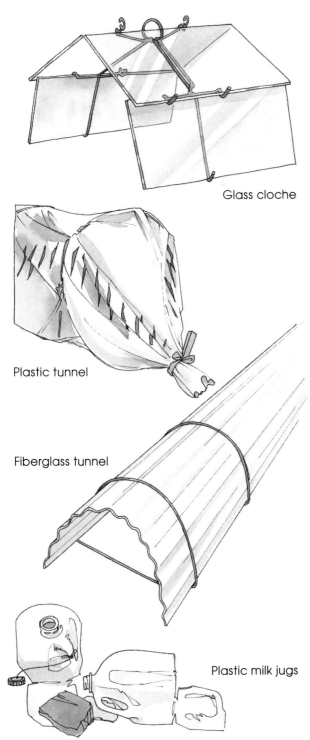

Glass cloche

Plastic tunnel

Fiberglass tunnel

Plastic milk jugs

Cloches for seedlings. Protect rows of young seedlings from cold temperatures with glass cloches or plastic or fiberglass tunnels. Cover individual plants with plastic milk jugs. Cut the bottom of the jug on three sides to form a flap. Set a rock on the flap to hold the jug in place. Put the cap on at night, but remove it during the day to avoid "cooking" the plant.

planting outdoors, and about 1½ acres are in production. One field was once a horse-riding ring; it was hard subsoil covered by 8 inches of sand. The other area was meadow grass over shale. In other words, the soil conditions are less than ideal.

Each year I throw whatever organic material I can find on the big sandy field and spread it as far as it will go. This field has gotten compost, mushroom soil, well-rotted horse manure, and sawdust from the barn floor. I also plant half of the field in buckwheat each year, alternating with the annuals and summer bulbs like glads. I till the crop under after it goes to seed, and it provides an inexpensive "green manure," adding organic matter and nutrient to the soil as it decomposes. (Buckwheat also produces fragrant white flowers that are a lovely addition to an informal fresh summer bouquet.) Gradually I've seen some improvement in the composition and drainage of the soil, and I no longer feel as if I'm planting my garden on the beach.

No matter what kind of soil you have in your garden, regular additions of compost and green manure crops can help loosen and enrich the earth and make your garden more productive and weed-free. In most cases you won't have to worry about the soil's pH (acidity or alkalinity), because the organic matter will help keep the soil well balanced. And as it breaks down, organic matter adds extra nutrients to the soil, so you won't need to add much extra fertilizer to keep the plants growing well. No matter what else you do to prepare your soil for planting, please don't skimp on the organic amendments!

General Garden Care

Once your seedlings are up and growing in the garden, there are a few things you'll want to do to help them stay vigorous and healthy. Watering and mulching are the two most important tasks, followed by other tasks like staking and controlling pests.

Watering

Too much water can cause roots to rot and plants to mildew—too little can stunt growth or kill plants outright. Of course, each plant has its own particular water needs. You'll save a lot of time and water if you try to match the plants you grow with the conditions you have available. In dry areas, try gray-leaved plants like artemisias

(*Artemisia* spp.) and lamb's-ears (*Stachys byzantina*). If you have a boggy spot, try yellow flag iris (*Iris pseudacorus*), which loves wet feet (and produces attractive seedpods for drying).

Fortunately, most of the plants that are good for crafting are adaptable to the moderately fertile, well-drained soil that other garden plants prefer. If you add plenty of organic matter to the bed before you plant, your flowers should do fine on about 1 inch of water a week, either from rainfall or irrigation.

Mulching

During the growing season, I use straw, newspaper, and black landscape fabric mulches to retain soil moisture and keep weeds down. (Other weed control strategies include rotary tilling between the beds three times a season and hand-weeding as necessary until the crop is tall enough to shade the soil.) Mulches also help keep the plants clean and prevent rain-splashed mud from getting on flowers.

Don't be in too much of a hurry to mulch—let the soil get warm and the plants get at least 4 to 6 inches tall before you start mulching. Adding a layer of finished compost around the plants before laying down other mulches is a good way to add some extra nutrients and organic matter to the soil.

Staking

I limit my staking efforts to four flowers: hollyhocks, delphiniums, peonies, and dahlias. The stems of these plants are often brittle, and a single strong storm can damage a whole crop. Staking also keeps weak-stemmed, heavy-flowered peonies from dropping into the mud. In my cutting garden, I surround the crowns of these plants with conical tomato cages in spring. The stems grow up within the cage, generally hiding it from view. In the decorative gardens closer to the house, I prefer using green-dyed bamboo stakes and tying up each plant individually. I permit other plants to find their own way, giving an informal appearance.

Controlling Pests

In matters of pest control, I prefer to maintain a laissez-faire attitude toward all insects except Japanese beetles. I've had good luck with leaving some weeds as decoys for the insects. Japanese beetles prefer wild cinquefoil (*Potentilla* spp.) to almost anything else I grow, so I let them

have it. I protect my roses and other plants by shaking off the beetles into a bucket of soapy water. Beetle traps put out by neighbors help by luring the pests away from my garden. If you use beetle traps yourself, place them well away from your beds so the powerful attractant doesn't lure them right to your prized specimens.

Avoiding Fall Garden Cleanup

Once again I admit that my actual practice runs contrary to customary good gardening advice. When the gardening column in the newspaper urges a fall cleanup to rid the garden of browned foliage and dead stems, I resist. I prefer to leave everything in place until spring, when the cleanup task is a pleasure rather than a chore. By procrastinating, I get more seedling "volunteers" in my garden, more tender plants that overwinter

Mulching for a great garden. *Spreading an organic mulch like straw around your plants helps the flowers stay clean and the roots stay cool and moist. Plus, it helps keep your weeding chores to a minimum!*

unexpectedly, and a natural system of markers to tell me where the herbaceous perennials are planted.

In early spring, I begin tidying up the garden by cutting off winter-damaged or dead leaves, along with the remaining dead stems. These materials, along with any tree leaves that may have accumulated in the beds, are a good base for the new season's compost pile.

Choosing Plants for Drying

There are hundreds of grasses, trees, shrubs, annuals, perennials, and biennials that are excellent for dried-flower crafts. And in your search for flowers, don't forget the wide range of leaves, pods, fruits, and stems that are also useful in a variety of projects. Look for plants that retain excellent form and color after being dried. Beige, brown, and other neutral tones are calming and peaceful in an arrangement, but the challenge in drying is to achieve vibrancy.

Garden Plants for Drying

Easy-to-grow perennials like bee balms, globe centaureas, globe thistles, artemisias, and yarrows form the mainstay of the dryer's garden. These dependable plants are long-lasting and relatively pest-free, producing more and more flowers each year. After you choose your perennials, fill in with brightly colored annuals like globe amaranths, strawflowers, and other everlastings. And while you're choosing plants, don't forget that trees and shrubs can also provide flowers, fruits, and other materials for crafts. "Garden Plants for Drying" on page 18 lists many plants that are ideal for use in a wide range of craft projects. Experiment with at least one or two new ones each year to find the ones that flourish in your growing conditions.

Wild Plants for Drying

Wildflowers, berries, grasses, leaves, and vines are readily available for collecting, allowing you to conserve precious garden space, cut down on your labor and expense, and expand the variety of materials that you work with. Even if you live in the downtown of a large city and have no garden, you can still find plenty of wild materials.

Grasses like green foxtail, which are commonly thought of as weeds, fight their way through cracks in sidewalk paving and can be plucked, when young and fresh, for drying. Goldenrod springs up uninvited in city planters and edges of parking lots. Abandoned lots harbor mullein, teasel, and cinquefoil. Highways are flanked with bittersweet vines choking out smaller trees. Purple loosestrife has become so invasive that it is being banned from sale and planting in several states. So when you see loosestrife splashing its vivid magenta in the wild marshes that you pass, you can cut some for drying without a twinge of guilt. Of course, you should always get permission from the landowner before cutting any plant material that's not on your property.

When picking in the wild you need to know which plants are scarce and protected, and which plants are poisonous. Avoid both with equal vigor. You can get lists of protected species from many sources, including your state's Department of Environmental Resources. Pictures and descriptions of poisonous plants are available in wildflower guide books. Besides helping you identify and stay away from dangerous plants, these guides can show you how to tell the poisonous plants from the useful ones. For example, if you know sumac only as a poisonous plant, you might neglect the staghorn and smooth sumacs, which are plentiful, easy to dry, and nonpoisonous.

Permanently stashed in my Jeep are a pair of pruning shears, gloves, and a collecting box. I never know when I'll spy something unusual growing by the side of the road and have to stop and snip a few pieces. In the days when my work attire included stockings and high heels, I also carried a pair of old boots in my collecting kit, to protect from runs and snags from roadside brambles. You'll find that it pays to be prepared for collecting at all times!

"Wildflowers to Dry" on page 21 shows my favorite wildflowers for drying. Many are useful garden plants as well, and you can get seed by gathering it from someone else's land (with their permission) or purchasing it. Several of these wildflowers are also available as plants at local nurseries, as seeds or plants in catalogs, or as cut flowers from your local florist. Many perennial catalogs, for example, offer goldenrod under its botanical name, *Solidago*. Goldenrod is also often available at your local florist as a cut flower imported from Holland.

Flowers from Other Sources

While there are many advantages to growing your own craft flowers, there are times when you

(continued on page 22)

GARDEN PLANTS FOR DRYING

It can be very difficult to decide exactly which plants you want to grow for drying. After all, you can dry most garden plants by one method or another, so theoretically your choices are limited only by your imagination and your willingness to experiment with different drying methods. In reality, though, you'll probably have to face the fact that you don't have room to grow all of the plants that you want.

Here I've listed some of the plants that I like best for drying. These plants are generally easy to grow in full sun and average, well-drained soil. Astilbes (*Astilbe* spp.), monkshoods (*Aconitum* spp.), and periwinkle (*Vinca minor*) benefit from partial shade and some extra moisture, while masterwort (*Astrantia major*) and pearly everlasting (*Anaphalis margaritacea*) appreciate a moist but sunny site. In areas where the temperature gets below the mid-twenties in winter, bring sweet bay (*Laurus nobilis*) indoors; the other plants on this list can take colder temperatures.

Since different catalogs and suppliers refer to plants by different names, alternate botanical and common names are given for some of the plants in the list. If you can't find a plant under its primary name, don't give up—try looking for it under its alternate name or its common name.

Botanical Name	Common Name	Color When Dried	Type
Achillea millefolium 'Summer Pastels'	'Summer Pastels' yarrow	White, orange, red, yellow, or lavender flowers	Perennial
Achillea × 'Moonshine'	'Moonshine' yarrow	Gold flowers	Perennial
Achillea ptarmica 'The Pearl'	'The Pearl' sneezeweed	White flowers	Perennial
Aconitum spp.	Monkshoods	Purple flowers	Perennial
Ageratum houstonianum 'Blue Horizon'	'Blue Horizon' ageratum	Lavender flowers	Annual
Alchemilla mollis	Lady's-mantle	Yellow-green flowers	Perennial
Allium spp.	Alliums	Lavender or white flowers	Perennial bulb
Amaranthus caudatus	Love-lies-bleeding	Wine-colored flowers	Annual
Amaranthus caudatus 'Green Thumb'	'Green Thumb' amaranth	Green flowers	Annual
Ammobium alatum	Winged everlasting	Pure white flowers	Annual
Anaphalis margaritacea	Pearly everlasting	White flowers	Perennial
Artemisia abrotanum	Southernwood	Green foliage	Perennial
Artemisia annua	Sweet wormwood, sweet Annie	Green foliage; gold flowers	Annual
Artemisia ludoviciana 'Silver King'	'Silver King' artemisia	Gray foliage	Perennial
Astilbe spp.	Astilbes	Pink flowers	Perennial
Astrantia major	Masterwort	Silver flower heads	Perennial
Belamcanda chinensis	Blackberry lily	Dark-purple seeds	Perennial
Buxus spp.	Boxwoods	Green foliage	Shrub
Calluna vulgaris 'H.E. Beale'	'H.E. Beale' heather	Pink flowers	Shrub
Cardiospermum halicacabum	Balloon vine, love-in-a-puff	Green seedpods	Annual
Carthamus tinctorius	Safflower	Green buds; orange flowers	Annual

Botanical Name	Common Name	Color When Dried	Type
Celosia cristata 'Century'	'Century' plumed celosia	Yellow, cream, red, or pink flowers	Annual
Celosia cristata 'Floradale' series	'Floradale' cockscomb	Pink, red, or yellow flowers	Annual
Centaurea cyanus 'Blue Boy'	'Blue Boy' bachelor's-button, 'Blue Boy' cornflower	Blue flowers	Annual
Centaurea macrocephala	Globe centaurea	Gold flowers	Perennial
Chrysanthemum pacificum	Gold-and-silver chrysanthemum	Yellow flowers	Perennial
Cortaderia selloana	Pampas grass	Pink flowers	Tender perennial
Cornus alba 'Sibirica'	Siberian dogwood	Red stems	Shrub
Corylus avellana 'Contorta'	Contorted hazel	Brown stems; greenish yellow catkins	Shrub
Craspedia globosa	Craspedia	Gold flowers	Perennial
Cytisus spp.	Brooms	Green stems	Shrub
Delphinium × *elatum* 'Pacific Giant' series	'Pacific Giant' delphiniums	Purple-blue flowers	Perennial
Echinacea purpurea	Purple coneflower	Mauve flowers	Perennial
Echinops ritro	Globe thistle	Blue-gray flower heads	Perennial
Eryngium spp.	Sea hollies	Blue-gray flower heads	Perennial
Gomphrena globosa	Globe amaranth	White, pink, or purple flowers	Annual
Gomphrena haageana	Orange globe amaranth	Orange or red flowers	Annual
Goniolimon tataricum, Limonium tataricum, Statice tatarica	German statice	White flowers	Perennial
Gypsophila paniculata 'Perfecta'	'Perfecta' baby's-breath	White flowers	Perennial
Helichrysum bracteatum	Strawflower	White, pink, salmon, red, or yellow flowers	Annual
Helipterum humboldtianum, Helipterum sandfordii	–	Bright gold flowers	Annual
Helipterum manglesii	Swan river everlasting, rhodanthe	Pink or white flowers	Annual
Helipterum roseum	Helipterum, acroclinium	Pink or white flowers	Annual
Heuchera sanguinea	Coral bells	Pink or rose flowers	Perennial
Hordeum vulgare	Barley	Green or beige seed heads	Annual
Humulus lupulus	Common hops	Green "cones"	Perennial
Hydrangea macrophylla 'Nikko Blue'	'Nikko Blue' hydrangea	True blue flowers	Shrub
Hydrangea paniculata 'Grandiflora'	Peegee hydrangea	Greenish to pink flowers	Shrub
Lagurus ovatus	Hare's-tail grass	Beige seed heads	Annual

(continued)

GARDEN PLANTS FOR DRYING—CONTINUED

Botanical Name	Common Name	Color When Dried	Type
Laurus nobilis	Sweet bay	Green leaves	Tender perennial
Lavandula angustifolia	Lavender	Lavender flowers; silvery leaves	Perennial
Leonotis leonurus	Lion's-ear	Orange flowers	Annual
Leontopodium alpinum	Edelweiss	White flowers	Perennial
Liatris scariosa	Tall gayfeather	Mauve flowers	Perennial
Limonium sinuatum	Annual statice	White, rose, salmon, purple, or yellow flower heads	Annual
Lonas annua	African daisy, golden ageratum	Gold flowers	Annual
Lunaria annua	Honesty, money plant	Pearly white inside green seedpods	Biennial
Mentha pulegium	Pennyroyal	Lavender flowers	Perennial
Moluccella laevis	Bells-of-Ireland	Green "flower" spikes	Annual
Monarda didyma 'Cambridge Scarlet'	'Cambridge Scarlet' bee balm	Deep-pink flowers	Perennial
Nepeta mussinii	Persian nepeta, catmint	Lavender flowers	Perennial
Nicandra physalodes	Apple-of-Peru, shoofly plant	Green to brown seedpods	Annual
Nigella damascena	Love-in-a-mist	Green-and-maroon striped seedpods	Annual
Nigella orientalis	Oriental fennel flower	Green seedpods	Annual
Origanum rotundifolium	—	Pale green leaves	Perennial
Paeonia spp.	Peonies	Pink or red flowers	Perennial
Papaver spp.	Poppies	Gray seedpods	Annual or perennial
Pennisetum setaceum	Fountain grass	Pink seed heads	Annual or perennial
Pentzia spp.	Pentzias	Gold flowers	Annual
Physalis alkekengi	Chinese lantern	Green or orange pods	Perennial
Proboscidea louisianica, Martynia proboscidea	Unicorn flower, martynia	Brown seedpods	Annual
Psylliostachys suworowii, Limonium suworowii, Statice suworowii	Rat-tail statice	Mauve flowers	Annual
Pycnanthemum tenuifolium	Mountain mint	Green leaves	Perennial
Rosa spp.	Roses	Red, pink, or white flowers; reddish fruit	Shrub
Rudbeckia hirta 'Double Gold'	'Double Gold' gloriosa daisy	Gold flowers with brown centers	Perennial
Salix caprea	Pussy willow	Silvery flowers	Shrub
Salix sachalinensis 'Sekka'	Japanese fantail willow	Brown stems	Tree
Salvia farinacea 'Blue Bedder'	'Blue Bedder' sage	Blue flowers	Annual or perennial
Salvia splendens 'Early Bonfire'	'Early Bonfire' scarlet sage	Red flowers	Annual

Botanical Name	Common Name	Color When Dried	Type
Santolina virens	Green lavender cotton	Green foliage	Perennial
Scabiosa stellata	–	Tan seed heads	Annual
Sedum × 'Autumn Joy'	'Autumn Joy' sedum	Mauve to chocolate brown flowers	Perennial
Sorghum bicolor	Sorghum	Brown-and-cream seed heads	Annual
Stachys byzantina	Lamb's-ears	Gray leaves and flower spikes	Perennial
Triticum aestivum	Wheat	Green or beige seed heads	Annual
Vinca minor	Periwinkle	Green foliage	Perennial
Viola × *wittrockiana*	Pansy	White, yellow, rose, orange, or purple-blue flowers	Annual
Wisteria spp.	Wisterias	Lavender flowers	Woody vine
Xeranthemum annuum	Immortelle	White, pink, or lavender flowers	Annual
Zinnia elegans 'Border Beauty'	'Border Beauty' zinnia	Rose flowers	Annual

WILDFLOWERS TO DRY

Many wild plants produce flowers, foliage, or pods that are wonderful for all kinds of crafts. Many of these plants are commonly thought of as weeds; some of them may already grow in your yard, whether you wanted them to or not. But don't ignore them just because you didn't plant them—think of these plants as free materials! If you plan to collect wildflowers from somewhere other than your property, be sure to get permission first. Many plants are known by more than one common name, so I've listed alternates where appropriate.

Botanical Name	Common Name	Part to Collect	Color When Dried
Asclepias tuberosa	Butterfly weed	Flowers; seedpods	Orange or yellow; brown
Celastrus scandens	American bittersweet	Seedpods; berries	Gold; orange
Daucus carota var. *carota*	Queen-Anne's-lace	Flowers	White
Dipsacus fullonum	Teasel	Seedpods	Green to brown
Echium vulgare	Viper's bugloss	Flowers	True blue
Eupatorium purpureum	Joe-Pye weed	Flowers	Mauve
Gnaphalium obtusifolium	Fragrant cudweed, sweet everlasting	Flowers	White
Iris pseudacorus	Yellow flag	Seedpods	Brown
Lepidium virginicum	Peppergrass	Seedpods	Greenish brown
Linaria vulgaris	Common toadflax, butter-and-eggs	Flowers	Yellow
Lythrum salicaria	Purple loosestrife	Flowers	Magenta

(continued)

WILDFLOWERS TO DRY—CONTINUED

Botanical Name	Common Name	Part to Collect	Color When Dried
Rhus glabra	Smooth sumac	Seed heads	Purplish red
Rosa multiflora	Multiflora rose	Fruit	Coral to red
Rumex acetosella	Sheep sorrel, sour dock	Seed heads	Green to pink or brown
Setaria spp.	Foxtails	Seed heads	Green
Solidago spp.	Goldenrods	Flowers; leaves	Gold; green
Tanacetum vulgare	Common tansy	Flowers	Gold
Verbascum spp.	Mulleins	Seed stalks	Brown

can't raise all of the plants that you want. Although I have an extensive garden, I do buy some fresh material I can't grow here, like proteas and eucalyptus, in order to reap the advantages of home drying. I may also purchase small bunches of flowers, leaves, or grasses to test-dry before I decide whether or not to try that plant in my garden. If I have a total crop failure, I have to buy from another grower who had better luck that year.

City dwellers without a garden, short-term renters, those who don't like to get dirty or to garden, or those whose time is too limited for gardening all can still dry their own flowers. Seek alternative sources of flowers and dry the blooms yourself, following the directions in the following chapter. You will be delighted at the quality you get with very little expenditure of effort. Here are some tips to keep in mind:

Buy fresh-cut flowers from your local farm stand, market, or florist. Dry them before they open too far or start to fade.

Purchase flowers for drying when they are "in season" to get the freshest material and the lowest prices. If you like larkspur or bachelor's-buttons, for example, you'll be more likely to find them at a reasonable price in the summer when these plants are blooming naturally in your area. While you may be able to find them at a florist's shop in December, the blooms will be much more expensive and the color selection will probably be limited. Make notes to tell yourself the proper timetable for the next year.

Approach neighbors who have flowers that you covet for drying, and play "Let's Make a Deal." Offer to buy or swap the blooms for something that you make or do, and see what happens. I've traded fresh-baked bread for honesty (*Lunaria annua*) and a cake for a hops vine. I have even stopped at doors of strangers and asked to buy flowers that seemed plentiful. To my surprise, I've never been refused. One woman even asked me to take a whole shrub of blue hydrangea, as she was tired of it and wanted to plant something else in its place. Of course, I obliged!

PICK RIGHT, DRY RIGHT

Dried flowers endure for millennia, according to archaeological evidence from the tombs of Egypt. At home, however, it is sufficient to save your flowers for several years. Even if the flower structure lasts, the colors gradually fade, both from exposure to light and because they gather a dust film. It's hard to notice this gradual dulling until you put the old flowers next to a new, freshly dried crop; just as you don't notice wallpaper fading until you take the pictures down from the walls at moving time. One of the advantages of growing and drying flowers yourself is that you can replace old arrangements with new dried materials any time you want to. Discarding an old design gives you the joy of creating a new one. Don't be practical—be lavish!

Harvesting for Drying

The goal of drying plant materials is to preserve their natural fresh color and form. To this end, how and when you harvest your flowers is as significant as how you dry them. Some flowers, like roses, are very forgiving—if you miss harvesting the flower buds, you can still harvest and dry the open flowers. Others, like goldenrod, need to be picked early, or they will not dry well. Below you'll find some simple guidelines that will help you harvest your materials at the right time for the best results.

Time of Day

Pick flowers for drying when all traces of dew, rain, or other moisture are gone. Unlike harvesting for fresh arrangements, picking flowers for drying is not an early-morning activity. You want the flowers and leaves to dry as rapidly as possible, and starting with dry flowers speeds up the process. In the heat of the summer, it's best to pick in late afternoon; that way, you'll avoid the wilting that accompanies a harvest during the broiling midday sun.

Ideally, you shouldn't harvest if it has just rained for several days. The plants will absorb extra moisture, and the flowers may not dry well. Sometimes, though, you may need to harvest even when the conditions aren't ideal. For example, if I have roses that need to be picked before they open too far, I cut them and shake off the excess water droplets. Then I bring the roses indoors and stand them in shallow buckets or vases of water. Within a few hours the rain has evaporated and I can bunch the stems for hanging. This technique works just as well for other flowers that you are determined to dry before you lose them.

Stage of Maturity

For the best-quality dried flowers, it's important to pick them at the proper stage of maturity. All too often, gardeners don't realize that even if a flower looks perfect in the garden, it may not keep that perfection when dried. Here are some general guidelines that will help you get the highest-quality dried flowers. "Harvesting Hints" on page 25 shows specific harvesting times for the most popular flowers.

Early Bloom

Some flowers, such as strawflowers (*Helichrysum bracteatum*), helipterums (*Helipterum* spp.), and winged everlastings (*Ammobium* spp.), continue to open even after they are picked, and the flower centers turn dark. If these flowers are nearly or fully open when you pick them, the dark center will detract from the flowers' appearance. If you pick the blooms as they are just starting to open, you will have the most attractive dried flowers.

Picking flowers before they are fully opened avoids another problem, commonly known as shattering. Shattering is the tendency of flower petals to fall at a touch or a breath of air. In nature, shattering helps plants to spread their seeds. When flowers of plants like Joe-Pye weed (*Eupatorium purpureum*), globe centaurea (*Centaurea macrocephala*), and goldenrod (*Solidago* spp.) are picked when open, their seeds continue to mature as they dry. After a few weeks in the house, the flowers will shatter into thousands of tiny seeds that fly all over your house. To avoid this catastrophe, pick these flowers as the buds just start to show color. The flowers will never mature beyond this stage and will stay as colorful dried buds.

Mid-Bloom

Beloved flowers like peonies and roses are often ruined in the drying process because they were picked too early or too late. If you pick them too early, the buds never open; if you pick them too late, the petals often brown and drop during the drying process. Harvest roses and peonies in the half-opened stage to prevent petals from dropping after air drying. When just fully opened, they can be successfully dried in silica gel, but you'll need to spray them with hair spray or a petal sealant product to keep them from drooping in humid weather.

Late Bloom

Several kinds of flowers dry best if you pick them when the flowers are fully open. Hydrangeas, for example, need to be picked when the petals feel papery and they rustle when touched, but before they start to turn brown. If picked too early, the petals will wither and not dry well.

Controlling the Colors

By changing the times you harvest certain materials, you can add many more colors to your dried-flower projects. In the garden, it's easy to see the progression of color from green buds to colorful open blooms. Experiment with collecting the flowers, fruits, or seeds at different stages, and you'll find that even one plant often provides at least two interesting colors when dried. "Pick for Changing Colors" on this page shows some plants that I pick at different stages in order to vary the color.

In the wild, seasonal color changes are often more subtle. A walk through fields in November reveals a variety of flower heads and seedpods in their final color stage: gray, brown, or black. These are not unattractive and have their place in your craft work. But also search for those same pods in July or August, and you can harvest lovely shades and tints of green for your arrangements.

Green is actually the hardest color to maintain when material is dried. Chlorophyll usually vanishes after three to six months, and yet it is the green in a dried arrangement or project that often changes it from a winterlike appearance to

PICK FOR CHANGING COLORS

Depending on when you pick, a single plant can often provide you with two or three different colors for your crafts. Here are some of the plants that I like to harvest at different times to get different colors.

Plant Name	Color Variations
Carthamus tinctorius (safflower)	Green buds; orange flowers
Centaurea macrocephala (globe centaurea)	Tan or gold calyxes; golden yellow flowers
Dipsacus fullonum (teasel)	Gray-green immature seedpods; brown when mature
Echinops ritro (globe thistle)	Gray young flower heads; blue when older
Hordeum vulgare (barley)	Green immature seed heads; beige when mature
Lunaria annua (honesty)	Green pods when unpeeled; opal with outer layer peeled off
Physalis alkekengi (Chinese lantern)	Green immature pods; orange when mature
Rhus typhina (staghorn sumac)	Pinkish immature seed heads; burgundy when mature
Rosa multiflora (multiflora rose)	Coral immature hips; red when mature
Rumex spp. (docks)	Green young seed heads; pink to brown when mature
Sedum × 'Autumn Joy' ('Autumn Joy' sedum)	Mauve young flowers; chocolate-colored when mature
Setaria spp. (foxtails)	Green immature seed heads; beige when mature
Solidago spp. (goldenrods)	Green leaves and buds; golden yellow flowers
Sorghum bicolor (sorghum)	Cocoa-colored flowers; ivory seeds
Triticum aestivum (wheat)	Green immature seed heads; beige when mature

a spring or summer one. In the garden, it's easy to find materials to pick and dry for their green color. However, wild pods and grasses in their green stage are camouflaged by hundreds of other species vying for attention. I make notes for myself

HARVESTING HINTS

Harvesting flowers at the right time is critical to drying them successfully. The list below shows when to harvest to get the best-quality dried flowers. If a flower doesn't appear on the table, pick it the first day it is fully open, before it starts to fade. Harvest pods as soon as they have reached the color you want—you don't have to wait until they are completely brown.

Buds (Color Showing)

Ammobium alatum (winged everlasting)
Anaphalis margaritacea (pearly everlasting)
Celastrus scandens (American bittersweet)
Centaurea macrocephala (globe centaurea)
Echinops ritro (globe thistle)
Eupatorium perfoliatum (boneset)
Eupatorium purpureum (Joe-Pye weed)
Solidago spp. (goldenrods)

Half Open

Ageratum spp. (ageratums)
Centaurea cyanus (bachelor's-button)
Consolida ambigua (rocket larkspur)
Delphinium spp. (delphiniums)
Helichrysum bracteatum (strawflower)
Liatris scariosa (tall gayfeather)
Lythrum salicaria (purple loosestrife)

Paeonia spp. (peonies)
Rosa spp. (roses)
Stachys byzantina (lamb's-ears)

Fully Open (Before Browning)

Achillea spp. (yarrows)
Allium spp. (alliums)
Celosia spp. (celosias)
Echinacea purpurea (purple coneflower)
Hydrangea spp. (hydrangeas)
Moluccella laevis (bells-of-Ireland)
Pentzia spp. (pentzias)
Rudbeckia hirta 'Gloriosa Daisy' (gloriosa daisy)
Salvia splendens (scarlet sage)
Tanacetum vulgare (common tansy)
Xeranthemum annuum (immortelle)

in a permanent garden calendar of where the wild mustard grows and where the teasel sprouts. Now my personal map and radar can lead me to hone in on my target even in the midst of its green disguise. If you watch the plants closely in the areas that you walk, you, too, will learn when and where to find these useful plants.

Freshness Counts

If you want the best dried flowers, you need to harvest and dry them when they are looking their best. Sometimes it is hard to remember this important fact. If your garden has produced a magnificent rose or delphinium, you may be (understandably) unwilling to hide it away in a dark drying area before it can be fully admired. Only you can decide whether you want to enjoy the flower fresh or dried.

If you decide to dry a flower, keep in mind that drying does not improve flower quality. The GIGO rule (Garbage In, Garbage Out) of computer jargon applies equally well to drying flowers. If you hang a faded, browning flower to dry, you'll get a faded, browned dried flower with petals ready to shatter at a touch. If you can steel your-self to pick flowers at their peak or dry gift flowers soon after you get them, you will get the finest-quality dried flowers that will last for years.

Drying Your Garden Bounty

Speed is essential in the drying process. You are in a race to preserve the flowers and leaves before they brown and die. There are four methods you can use: air drying, desiccant drying, microwave drying, and pressing. Many people ask me if they can freeze-dry flowers at home. Unfortunately, the freeze-drying machines now on the market are much too expensive for the home gardener. If you buy flowers that have been freeze-dried, spray them with protectant like hair spray (as you would desiccant-dried flowers) to prevent them from reabsorbing moisture from the air.

Air Drying

Air drying is a simple process that allows moisture in the plant material to evaporate naturally. To air dry flowers, bunch six to ten stems together and hang them upside down from a wire, line, or hook. The exact length of time it takes the

FABULOUS DRIED FRUITS

If you're looking for unusual materials to dry, don't neglect the wide range of fruits available in your yard or at your local supermarket. Many of these fruits are easy to dry, and they add a unique touch to any craft. I slice many fruits thinly and dry them in a 200°F oven for several hours. Then I set the fruits to dry the rest of the way in a warm place: near the furnace or on top of the refrigerator, for example. I use an old window screen in the basement and cookie racks on top of my kitchen radiator for drying in winter. Here are pointers for some of my favorite fruits.

Apples. Cut unpeeled 'Red Delicious' apples in thin slices. Slice horizontally to get the star pattern in the middle or vertically to get the apple silhouette. Soak slices immediately in a solution of 2 quarts of water, 2 tablespoons of lemon juice, and 2 tablespoons of Fruit Fresh (available in the canning section of your market). Remove the slices after 15 minutes, pat dry with a paper towel, and bake on a cookie sheet lined with waxed paper at 200°F for 2 hours. Turn them frequently, and keep checking to make sure they don't brown. Remove the slices when they feel leathery, and continue drying them on a cookie rack in a warm spot.

Mushrooms. Start with extra-large stuffing mushrooms—they will shrink as they dry. Dry mushrooms on a cookie rack in a warm place (which takes about three weeks) or in a 200°F oven for 2 to 3 hours, until they feel dry. In the oven, be sure to place a drip pan beneath them since they exude moisture as they dry.

Oranges, lemons, and grapefruit. Slice thinly and dry the fruit on a cookie sheet in a *very* low oven (about 200°F) for 2 to 3 hours. Turn the fruit several times during the drying process. Remove the slices from the oven before they are brown, and let them finish drying on a cookie rack.

Osage oranges. Slice thinly; discard the ends. Bake in a 200°F oven for 3 to 4 hours and finish drying on a cookie rack. They will turn a lovely golden brown as they dry.

Pomegranates. Cut off the bottom third, leaving the blossom end on the bigger piece. Scoop out the seeds and juice into a bowl: eat these later as a treat. Rinse the shells under clear water, and dry with a paper towel. Place on a cookie rack to dry—they don't need to be oven-dried. They should be ready in about one week.

---

plants to dry depends on the kind of plant, the quantity you have to dry, the maturity of the material, and the temperature and humidity of the drying area. Fleshy succulents like sedums will take much longer to dry than feathery gray artemisias or delicate flowers like larkspur. Huge canna leaves take about four weeks to air dry completely; strawflowers only take about five days in a warm spot. Figure on at least a week to dry most flowers.

Choosing a Drying Area

Search for a spot in your home that is dark, dry, and warm—perhaps an attic, basement, closet, or garage. In my house, the best spot is in the furnace room, where the mammoth antique water heater provides heat even throughout the summer. When the plumber comes on his yearly cleaning schedule, he must part curtains of drying peo-

nies or delphiniums dangling from wires strung above the furnace.

I dry most of the flowers at the Meadow Lark in the barn, where they are dependent on the vagaries of summer humidity. During one drought year, flower production was reduced about 25 percent, but the drying results were magnificent. The wettest summer on record led to abundant growth, but drying was slow and some fading was inevitable. Relax and do the best you can with the conditions you have.

Leaving the Leaves

Most books recommend stripping all leaves from a stem before drying. The theory is that moisture evaporating into the air from the leaves may affect the general atmospheric humidity, thus slowing the drying time of the flower. The first two years I dried flowers in quantity, I assidu-

The best hang-ups. *When you are looking for a place in your home to air dry flowers, consider the attic, the garage, or another warm, dark, dry place. At the Meadow Lark, the area around the antique hot water heater is a perfect spot for hanging flowers to dry.*

ously followed this general wisdom. Not only did my fingers have a permanent chlorophyll stain from stripping quantities of leaves, but my flowers looked like plucked chickens. A yarrow stem devoid of leaves looks naked. Dried flower arrangements without green look desolate and wintery.

I discovered through trial and error that there is absolutely no need to strip all of the leaves. Keep bunches small (with six to ten stems each), spread them out (with 6 inches between hanging bunches), and provide the drying room with some air circulation (perhaps by keeping a door open), and you can retain all the green you want. Cockscombs (*Celosia* spp.), roses, hydrangeas, sorghum (*Sorghum bicolor*), and yarrows have particularly green foliage when dried. Lavender foliage is gray but useful for its fragrance.

Preparing Plants for Drying

Rubber bands are the only effective tool for bunching the stems, because the bands contract as the stems shrink in diameter. If you use string or yarn to tie the bunches, you usually end up with a floor full of material that has slipped out of the bunch when dry. Simply wrap the rubber band around the stems until it holds them together securely. An ordinary paper clip spread open is a cheap and effective hanging hook. To hang the material to dry, slip one end of the paper clip through the rubber band, and the other around a hook, wire, or line.

Air-dried bunches are easy to suspend upside down from a wire, but some large, flat flowers will shrivel and close when hung in this manner. To dry gloriosa daisies (*Rudbeckia hirta* 'Gloriosa Daisy'), purple coneflowers (*Echinacea purpurea*), and Queen-Anne's-lace (*Daucus carota* var. *carota*), I use an old window screen with holes punched in it. Lay the screen flat across a tomato cage or other prop, and poke each flower stem down through a hole, with the petals or the base of the flower head resting flat on top of the screen. The flowers will dry in this position and will not curl up after you remove them from the screen.

True everlastings, such as strawflowers and globe amaranths, air dry equally well by several different methods of air drying. Hang bunches of flowers with leaves on their natural stems; harvest and dry the flower heads on a screen or tray; or wire the freshly harvested flower heads for future arrangements.

Wiring is extremely simple if you use a "bright" stub wire, available at most craft shops or garden centers that sell floral supplies. (For more information on "bright" stub wire and other craft materials, see Appendix C on page 147.) Stick the wire tip about halfway through the calyx (base) of the flower and stand the completed flowers in a jar. As the flowers dry, the wire inside rusts slightly, and the flowers shrink around the roughened wire, producing a tight, secure bond. I never use the green wire commonly sold in craft

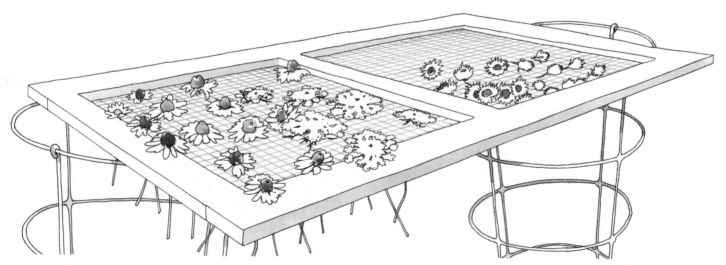

Window screen drying rack. Old window screens are perfect for supporting flowers like Queen-Anne's-lace while they dry. Screens are also a good place to dry stemless flower heads for later use.

Drying on the spot. *To minimize crumbling and waste, some-times you can pick plants fresh and let them dry right in a craft. Pussy willow, bittersweet, hydrangea, bells-of-Ireland, and many herbs dry well this way. (See the Culinary Herb Wreath project on page 66 for details on how to construct this wreath.)*

stores for this purpose because I've found that the flower heads will slip off the coated wire unless you make a tiny hook at the end of the wire and pull it down into the flower head—a process which often damages the flowers.

Desiccant Drying

Desiccants are materials like sand, silica gel, cat box litter, and cornmeal that can absorb moisture from plant tissues. I have tried all of these materials, and by far the best of the desiccants is silica gel, which is a white sandlike material packaged for floral use. It is not cheap, but you can reuse it for many years by drying it when it becomes saturated. Manufacturers usually mix in small colored particles with the silica gel as moisture indicators. The particles are blue when dry, pink when saturated.

Preparing the Flowers

The part of the flower that you actually dry depends on the type of flower and what you plan to use it for. For most flowers, you'll just want to bury the bloom itself, so cut off the rest of the stem about a half an inch below the base of the flower. Save stems to air dry and reuse; dry leaves separately as desired. For flowers with a hollow stem or calyx like delphiniums, zinnias, and marigolds, you can reinsert a stem into the hollow base of the flower after drying. I save extra-stiff stems to use for this purpose.

If you think you might use the flower in a long-stemmed arrangement, insert a 5-inch piece of stub wire through the calyx, and allow it to extend out both sides. I treat roses, peonies, carnations, and lilies in this way. Bury the flower and wire together. Later when you are ready to use the flower, you can easily attach the wire to a floral pick or a stem.

If you have tall, spiky flowers like foxgloves (*Digitalis* spp.), delphiniums, and snapdragons, lay them down on a bed of silica gel in a long container, then bury them gently. The flowers on the back of the stalk will get slightly crushed in the drying process, so make sure you keep the good side facing front when you use the spike in a craft.

Using Silica Gel

Before starting, I always put on a face mask or respirator—I figure the fine particles can't be good for my lungs. All brands of silica gel include simple directions for use. The basic procedure

starts with placing the flower head upright in a half-inch of silica gel. Then gradually pour the silica gel around the outside of the flower, forming a mound that will support the petals and prevent them from flattening out. After the mound is built up, gently pour the silica gel on top of the flower to bury it completely. If you are willing to take the time, spooning extra gel into funnel- or pouch-shaped flowers before covering them will help the blooms keep their shape while drying.

If the silica gel was relatively dry when you started, your flowers will be ready in one to two weeks. Fortunately, it doesn't do them any harm if you forget them, as I usually do, and leave them buried for months. Gently pour off the silica gel to save for another day, and blow remaining particles off the petals.

After using the silica gel several times, the blue crystals will turn pinkish, telling you it's

Drying in silica gel. Place rounded flowers like roses on a base of about an inch of silica gel. Use a spoon to pour more desiccant around the flower until it is completely covered.

time to redry the material. Pour the gel into a shallow baking pan, place the uncovered pan in a 200°F oven, and stir every 20 minutes. Check after 1 hour to see if the indicator crystals are blue again. If not, keep stirring and checking the gel until you see that the crystals are blue. (After many, many uses the indicator crystals may lose their color entirely. By that time, though, you'll have a good feeling for when the gel needs to be dried.) Remove the pan from the oven, and cover it with foil to prevent the gel from absorbing water vapor from the air while it is cooling. Store the gel in a sealed container until you are ready to use it.

Protecting Desiccant-Dried Flowers

If you are not using the flowers immediately, store them in a single layer in a covered container. After arranging flowers dried with desiccants, apply a protective spray like petal sealer or hair spray lightly over the surface to help seal out humidity. Some museums store dried-flower arrangements during the humid periods of the summer and return them to display when the heat is switched on again in the fall—you may want to try this at home.

Pressing

Pressing is an easy and attractive way to preserve the beauty of many kinds of leaves and flowers. Pressed flowers need a warm, dry atmosphere in order to retain their vibrant colors. They must be heavily weighted in order to dry flat and smooth. For a few small flowers, a weighted telephone book will suffice. But if you have more flowers, a flower press is most practical.

Making the Press

You can purchase a flower press or you can make one yourself from scrap lumber. My favorite press is made from two pieces of ½-inch-thick unpainted plywood. It is 12 inches wide and 20 inches long. I drilled a hole in each corner, ½ inch from the edge, and used 2-inch-long bolts and wing nuts to tighten the press.

Press your flowers between layers of absorbent paper, like blotter paper or blank newsprint. You can reuse blotter paper indefinitely once it is dry. Beware of colored or inky papers, which will bleed dye onto the flowers. Also avoid embossed papers, like napkins or toweling, that will impress little designs into the flowers. Placing corrugated cardboard between the paper layers helps absorb more moisture.

Filling the Press

Just as with other methods of drying, the goal of pressing flowers is to preserve as much of the natural color as you can. Following the steps below will help you get the best possible dried flowers.

1. Gather plant material when it is dry. Avoid picking flowers the day after a very heavy rain when the plants have absorbed a lot of water. Also avoid collecting flowers that are wet with dew.

2. Pick whole flowers, petals, leaves, and tendrils. Pick flowers in different stages of development: buds, half-open and fully open flowers, and seed heads. Select only "perfect" flowers for pressing; flowers don't improve in the press. Don't overlook tiny weeds and grasses that may add interest to your craft work.

FAVORITES FOR DESICCANT DRYING

Silica gel is an easy and effective way to preserve almost any flower. For some very delicate flowers, it is the only way to preserve them successfully. Orchids, daisies, and dogwood blossoms are all good candidates for desiccant drying. Here's a list of some other flowers that I dry in silica gel.

Aster spp. (asters)
Dianthus caryophyllus (florist's carnation)
Digitalis spp. (foxgloves)
Helleborus spp. (hellebores)
Iris spp. (irises)
Lilium spp. (lilies)

Narcissus spp. (daffodils)
Rosa spp. (roses, fully open)
Tagetes spp. (marigolds, large)
Tulipa spp. (tulips)
Zantedeschia spp. (calla lilies)
Zinnia elegans (zinnia, large)

3. In the open press, place a layer of corrugated cardboard, a layer of blotting paper, a single layer of flowers, and another layer of blotting paper. Continue adding new layers of cardboard, paper, and flowers until you fill the press. All of the flower parts in a plant layer should be the same size so that the layer will be the same thickness throughout. Avoid crowding—items should lie at least 1 inch from each other on the paper.

4. Finish the stack with corrugated cardboard and the top of the press. Tighten the press with the wing nuts.

5. Retighten the press *every day* until you no longer can. As the flowers dry and moisture evaporates, there will be extra space between the layers. If you don't continue to retighten the press, the flowers may wrinkle as they dry.

6. After the third day, change the blotter paper and replace with fresh, dry paper. This will prevent mildew and browning. Carefully lift each flower with the tip of a knife and reposition it on the new dry paper layers.

7. How do you know when flowers are dry? There is no harm in peeking. How fast they dry depends on the thickness of the flower, its moisture content, how densely you pack the material on each layer in the press, how many layers there are, the absorbency of the paper, and the warmth and dryness of the room where you store the press. When you change the paper, as in Step 6, flowers dry about 75 percent faster. When dry, the petals or leaves should feel papery and make a rustling noise.

8. Store pressed flowers between layers of waxed paper in a box or cabinet away from light and humidity, the two banes of all dried flowers.

Microwave Drying

I occasionally dry flowers in a microwave, but I prefer not to. Microwaving is a time-consuming technique, especially if you have lots of flowers to dry, because you can only process a few flowers at a time. You also should expect to overcook some flowers until you figure out just how long that kind of flower needs to dry. A microwave-dried flower can be dried, cooled, and ready to use in about 1 hour—instead of having to spend a week in silica gel in the closet. If you need dried flowers for a craft in a hurry, and you have some to waste in experimenting with heating times, give this technique a try.

Total drying times for both flowers and leaves depend on the power of your microwave, the number of items you dry at a time, and the size, moisture content, and maturity of the plant materials. No matter what instructions you use for microwave drying, you'll have to experiment with each type of flower and leaf until you get the results you want. When you are drying plant material in the microwave, keep a close eye on the microwave at all times, and stop the process if the leaves or flowers look or smell burnt.

If you plan to wire your flowers, wait until *after* drying, because you can't put metal in the microwave. You *can* put a wooden toothpick up through the base of the flower, and use it to anchor a wire when arranging the flowers later. Following the instructions for regular desiccant drying

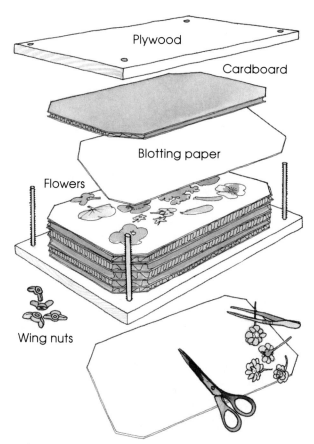

Layers of a flower press. It's easy to make and use a flower press. Just assemble the press with the layers shown above, and add a variety of small flowers and grasses. Remember that small, thin materials dry best; for large flowers like zinnias, remove the petals and press them individually.

SUCCESS WITH PRESSED FLOWERS

Pressed flower projects are fun and easy when you have plenty of materials to choose from. Take the time to collect many different flowers and leaves during the growing season, and you'll be able to create a wide range of beautiful crafts. Here are some tips to help you get perfect pressed flowers.

• Press more material than you need for your project. You'll want to discard the crinkled or broken pieces after pressing.

• When you add materials to your press, make a note of the date and the contents on the cover of the press. You think you'll remember what's inside; but after a month or so, you probably won't. This way, you won't have to keep opening and closing the press.

• Choose a variety of colors. Even if you plan to make a monochromatic design, a touch of contrasting color can add zip.

• Flowers that air dry well also keep their colors well in pressing. Oranges and yellows stay around for years; whites and greens are the hardest to keep.

• For long-lasting pure white flowers, press white everlastings like winged everlasting (*Ammobium alatum*) and immortelle (*Xeranthemum annuum*).

• For the best greens, try pressing the mature leaves of English ivy (*Hedera helix*), roses, yarrows, and cosmos.

on page 30, bury the plant material in silica gel in an uncovered microwave-safe plastic, ceramic, or glass bowl. Place the bowl in the microwave, along with a small cup or bowl of water. Heat the gel on high power for about 2 minutes, and then let it set in the microwave for an additional few minutes. Remove the silica gel bowl from the microwave and cover it with a lid left slightly ajar to let any moisture escape while the gel cools. Also, don't forget to wipe any accumulated moisture out of your microwave with a paper towel after each use.

Once the silica gel is cool to the touch, pour it off into another container and gently remove the flower. It should be bright and slightly crisp. If it is brittle or dark, try heating the next one about 30 seconds less. If the flower is limp, try heating it 30 seconds longer. Experiment with different drying times until you get the results you want, and then record the time for that type of flower for future reference.

Leaves are easy to dry in the microwave without silica gel. Put one or two leaves on a microwave-safe paper towel into the oven along with a cup of water, and heat on high for about 1 minute. Properly dried leaves are stiff but not brittle or brown. If the leaves are not fully dry by this time, heat them again for 30 seconds; if they're too dry, heat the next batch 30 seconds less. Keep track of the total drying time for each kind of leaf for your next drying session. If you like to learn more about microwave drying, I suggest you get a copy of Titia Joosten's *Flower Drying with a Microwave*.

A Gallery of Dried Flowers

On the following pages you'll find photographs of dried flowers arranged by color. Use them to help you choose materials to fit a color scheme, or to identify unusual materials that you would like to grow.

"Yellows, Golds, and Oranges" shows the range of bright, sunny colors available for your dried arrangements. Use the bright yellow of globe centaurea, creamy yellow of cockscomb, or the orangey yellow of gloriosa daisies to add a vibrant, cheerful touch to your crafts.

"Pinks and Reds" displays some of the warmer shades available in dried flowers. Try the deep maroon of sumac seedheads, the bright red of scarlet sage, or the rich, velvety red of cockscomb to give your crafts a warm feeling. Or create a delicate-looking arrangement with pale or creamy pink flowers.

"Blues and Purples" offers some of the most popular colors for flower crafts. From the icy silver-blue of globe thistle to the vibrant magenta of globe amaranth, this color group can provide a wide range of effects to your craft work.

"Greens and Neutrals" shows just a few of the neutral-colored materials available for craft projects. The silvery flower stalks of lamb's-ears and mullein, airy sprays of German statice, and striped pods of okra all add texture and interest to any wreath or arrangement.

YELLOWS, GOLDS, AND ORANGES

Chrysanthemum parthenium (Feverfew)

Helipterum humboldtianum

Rosa spp. (Roses)

Sorghum bicolor (Broomcorn)

Heliopsis helianthoides (Oxeye)

Leonotis leonurus (Lion's-ear)

Solidago spp. (Goldenrods)

Craspedia globosa (Craspedia)

Alchemilla mollis (Lady's-mantle)

Calendula officinalis (Pot marigold)

Physalis alkekengi
(Chinese lantern)

Carthamus tinctorius (Safflower)

Achillea
× 'Moonshine'
('Moonshine' yarrow)

Santolina virens (Green lavender cotton)

Rudbeckia hirta
'Gloriosa Daisy'
(Gloriosa daisy)

Centaurea macrocephala
(Globe centaurea)

Tanacetum vulgare
(Common tansy)

Helianthus annua
(Sunflower)

Gomphrena haageana
(Orange globe amaranth)

Celosia cristata
(Cockscomb)

Rosa spp. (Roses)

PINKS AND REDS

Sedum × 'Autumn Joy' ('Autumn Joy' sedum)

Gomphrena 'Strawberry Fields' ('Strawberry Fields' globe amaranth)

Monarda didyma 'Cambridge Scarlet' ('Cambridge Scarlet' bee balm)

Salvia splendens (Scarlet sage)

Zinnia elegans (Zinnia)

Consolida ambigua (Rocket larkspur)

Rubus sp. (Black raspberries)

Celosia cristata (Plumed celosia)

Rosa spp. (Roses)

Helichrysum bracteatum (Strawflower)

Rubus spp. (Blackberries)

Helipterum roseum
(Helipterum)

Heuchera sanguinea
(Coral bells)

Limonium sinuatum
(Annual statice)

Rhus spp. (Sumacs)

Dahlia spp. (Dahlias)

Gomphrena globosa
(Globe amaranth)

Paeonia lactiflora (Peony)

Celosia cristata (Cockscomb)

Hydrangea paniculata 'Grandiflora'
(Peegee hydrangea)

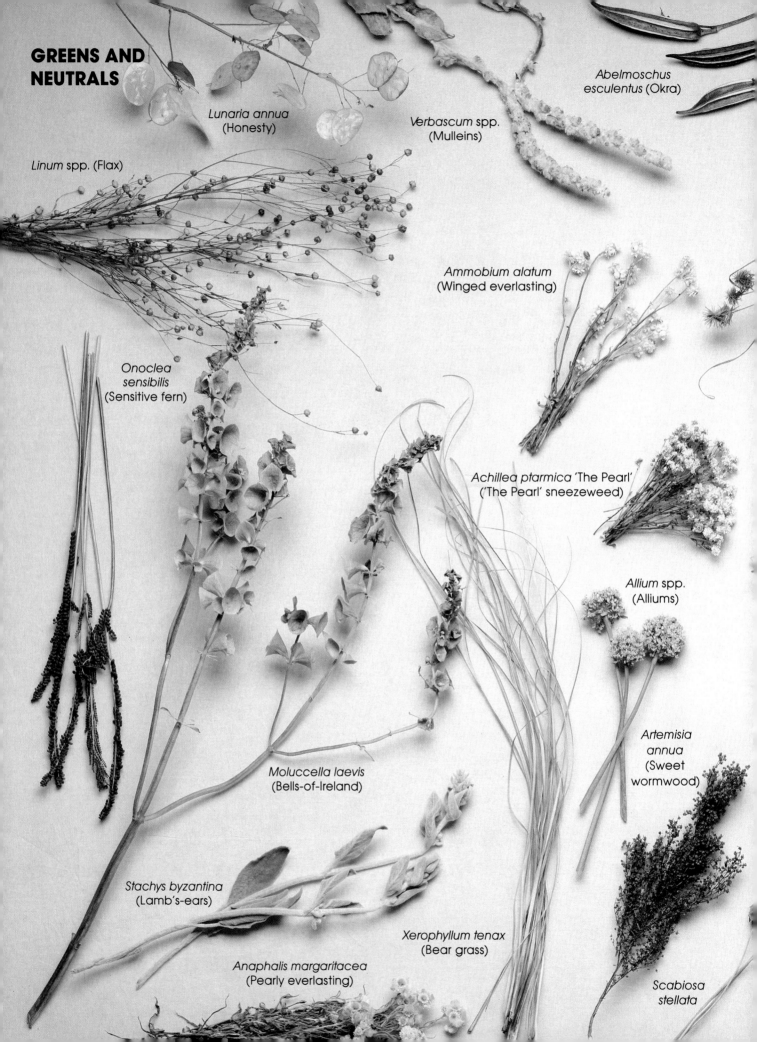

GREENS AND NEUTRALS

Lunaria annua (Honesty)

Verbascum spp. (Mulleins)

Abelmoschus esculentus (Okra)

Linum spp. (Flax)

Ammobium alatum (Winged everlasting)

Onoclea sensibilis (Sensitive fern)

Achillea ptarmica 'The Pearl' ('The Pearl' sneezeweed)

Allium spp. (Alliums)

Artemisia annua (Sweet wormwood)

Moluccella laevis (Bells-of-Ireland)

Stachys byzantina (Lamb's-ears)

Xerophyllum tenax (Bear grass)

Anaphalis margaritacea (Pearly everlasting)

Scabiosa stellata

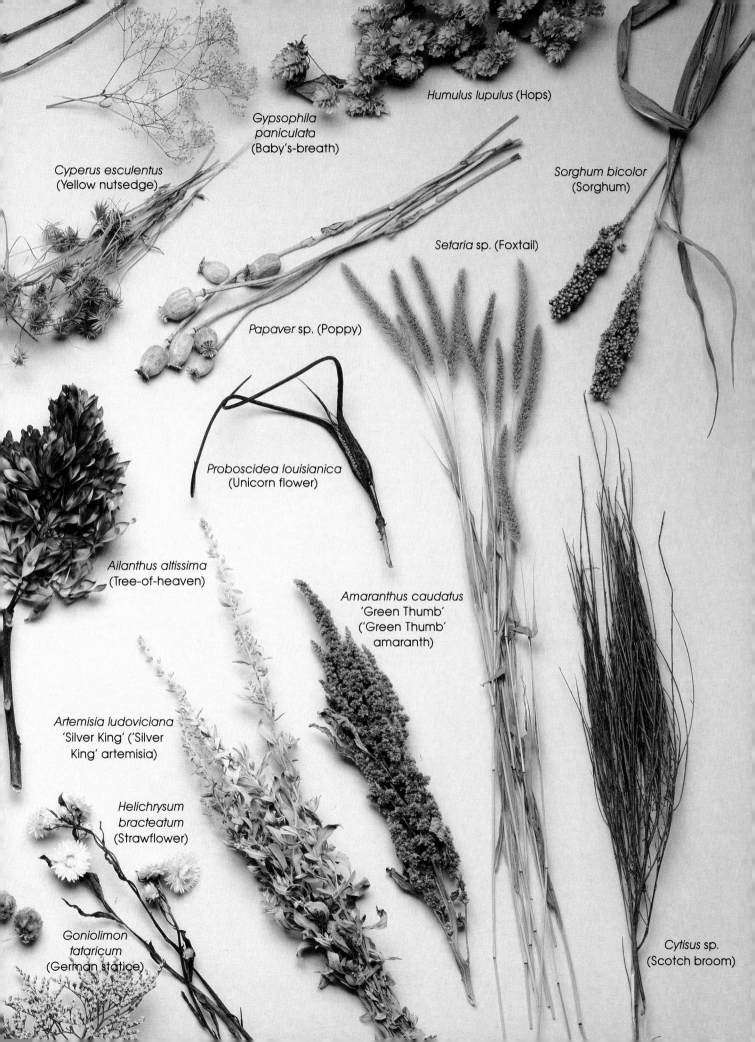

Humulus lupulus (Hops)

Gypsophila paniculata (Baby's-breath)

Cyperus esculentus (Yellow nutsedge)

Sorghum bicolor (Sorghum)

Setaria sp. (Foxtail)

Papaver sp. (Poppy)

Proboscidea louisianica (Unicorn flower)

Ailanthus altissima (Tree-of-heaven)

Amaranthus caudatus 'Green Thumb' ('Green Thumb' amaranth)

Artemisia ludoviciana 'Silver King' ('Silver King' artemisia)

Helichrysum bracteatum (Strawflower)

Goniolimon tataricum (German statice)

Cytisus sp. (Scotch broom)

BLUES AND PURPLES

Eryngium spp. (Sea hollies)

Lythrum salicaria (Purple loosestrife)

Wisteria spp (Wisterias)

Psylliostachys soworowii (Rat-tail statice)

Gomphrena globosa (Globe amaranth)

Limonium sinuatum (Annual statice)

Centaurea cyanus (Cornflower)

Mentha pulegium (Pennyroyal)

Amaranthus caudatus (Love-lies-bleeding)

Verbena hastata (Blue vervain)

Nigella damascena pods and flowers (Love-in-a-mist)

Paeonia lactiflora (Peony)

Eupatorium purpureum
(Joe-Pye weed)

Origanum spp. (Marjoram)

Dahlia spp. (Dahlias)

Armeria maritima
(Common thrift)

Echium vulgare
(Viper's bugloss)

Monarda citriodora
(Lemon mint)

Xeranthemum annuum
(Immortelle)

Echinops ritro
(Globe thistle)

Delphinium × *elatum*
(Delphinium)

Mentha suaveolens
(Apple mint)

*Hydrangea
macrophylla*
'Nikko Blue' ('Nikko
Blue' hydrangea)

Salvia farinacea
(Blue sage)

Ageratum houstonianum
'Blue Horizon' ('Blue
Horizon' ageratum)

THE SPRING GARDEN

There are a few warm days in late winter when the moist, earthy smell in the air propels me into the garden. The temptation to remove the mulch and accumulated debris so I can see the tiny green shoots is almost overwhelming, although I know that it is too early to start a full cleanup. Walking on the soil when it is too wet would compact the earth, making it difficult for the tender, new plant roots to develop properly. And removing the cozy winter mulch too early would leave the succulent new shoots to face the next brutal cold snap unprotected. I know I must exercise heroic restraint and start on my indoor work instead.

For me, the first big project of the year is starting seeds. Growing your own plants from seed is both an exciting challenge and a great way to save money. This process also lets you choose new or unusual plants that are not available for sale on a commercial basis.

I usually start planting slow-growers like delphiniums by mid-January. As soon as I return from my 11-day stint at the Philadelphia Flower Show in mid-March, I begin planting the rest of the seeds. I try not to plant the fast-growing annuals too early; six weeks before the last frost is usually enough of a head start.

By mid-spring, the first new flowers and grasses are ready to be harvested, dried, and pressed for use in projects for the new season. In my garden, pansies are the first flower to be pressed, followed closely by grape hyacinths and wild mustard. Sometimes it's hard to decide whether to enjoy the spring flowers fresh or to dry them for later use. I struggle with the two sides of my nature: one wants to keep the armloads of perfumed peonies to enjoy in the house, and one wants to hang them all immediately in the furnace room where they will dry quickly and retain their color. I compromise and keep the whites for fresh arrangements, while the pinks and reds (which dry better than the white ones) get bunched and hung.

It's even harder to cut the few Dutch irises that have been left by the deer, but I want some to dry in silica gel for an oriental-style arrangement, and there is only a limited time for harvesting. The flowers start to fade soon after they are fully open, and you must catch them while the purple is still vibrant. I pick some leaves as well as the flower stems, trying not to denude the plant—the bulbs remaining need the leaves to collect nutrients for next year's flowers.

As the new season begins, be on the lookout for all kinds of foliage that might be suitable for your crafts. Thanks to Gary Koller and Nan Sinton of the Arnold Arboretum, my eye is newly attuned to the color nuances in leaves. In an intensive three-day course on shrubs and perennials, these talented teachers changed the way I perceive the universe and design a garden. Now there are times when I choose a plant for the shape and texture of the foliage, regardless of the appeal of the flower. Variegated foliage, with its outlines of white or yellow, can accent plantings throughout much of the year. Try selecting plants with red, blue, or yellow tints in their leaves to highlight nearby shrubs or flowers. Experiment with drying the leafy treasures that you find, and enjoy their beauty for months to come.

❧ Spring Bonnet

It's easy to turn a plain hat into something special—just add a few flowers! To create your own masterpiece, start with a comfortable straw hat in an attractive color and shape. Then select materials to complement the color and style of the hat, plus white and green for a bit of contrast. Between wearings, store your creation in a spot that needs a splash of color—a hallway, or perhaps a bedroom.

WHAT YOU NEED

20 sprigs of German statice

8 pieces of pink celosia

20 strawflower heads (an assortment of salmon, red, white, and yellow)

6 rosebuds with leaves

1 stem of pink larkspur, broken into pieces

8 feet of wired ribbon, 1½ inches wide

6 inches of thin wire

Scissors

Straw hat

Hot glue gun and glue sticks, or thick white craft glue

WHAT YOU DO

1. Cut a piece of ribbon long enough to go around the base of the hat's crown, about 2 feet. Set aside the remaining ribbon.

2. Wrap the shorter piece of ribbon around the base of the crown, and glue the two ends to the hat in the middle of the back. You may also need a touch of glue in the front to keep the ribbon in place.

3. Make a bow using the rest of the ribbon and the wire, and glue it to the middle of the back of the hat, on top of the ribbon band. See Appendix A on page 144 for instructions on making a bow.

4. Attach the dried materials with glue—statice first, then larger flowers like celosia and strawflowers. Finish with the small flowers, like rosebuds, in places they will show up best. Glue some of the floral material to the ribbon, some to the brim, and some to the base of the crown. Don't skimp on the flowers, but allow some of the ribbon to peek through for additional color.

Variations: Tailor the floral design to the hat design, as I did with the hats in the photo on the opposite page. I like to encircle a wide-brimmed hat, like the red one, with floral material. The yellow fedora gets a jaunty air from its feathery spike of black-bearded wheat, complemented by a yellow-and-white striped ribbon, yellow and gold strawflowers, poppy pods, yellow statice, and *Helipterum humboldtianum.* To perk up an otherwise plain white boater, I added a deep-blue rib-

bon bow and trimmed the hat with globe thistles, German statice, maroon strawflowers, winged everlastings, helipterums, and globe amaranths.

PROJECT POINTERS

Growing

Sow the lovely annual larkspur (*Consolida ambigua*) directly where it is to grow. Plant the seeds early in the spring for bloom later in the summer, or plant seeds in late summer to get flowers early the following spring.

Harvesting

In all of your dried-flower designs, consider working with flowers at different stages of development: some in bud, some slightly more open, some in the seedpod stage. Even though you have worked hard to grow large blooms, you should pick some buds and some smaller flowers as they are just starting to open to keep for crafts.

Drying

Rosebuds appear everywhere when you are searching for them. If you don't have any in your own garden, a friend might spare a bud or two, or a florist on Saturday might be willing to part with a few of her leftovers at little or no cost. Sweetheart or miniature roses also look terrific when dried. Dry them on a cake rack on top of your refrigerator. If you have a built-in refrigerator with the air vent near the top, hang one or two buds upside down by inserting the stems in the grille.

Bedecked Basket and Candle Bobeches

Flowers are perfect complements to baskets and candles. The Bedecked Basket (*left*) is a good way to use your "brokies"—the lovely intact flower heads that have had their stems broken off in the harvesting or drying process. The Candle Bobeches, or candle rings, (*right*) are a charming way to combine candles and flowers.

Bedecked Basket

WHAT YOU NEED

2 to 3 handfuls of green sheet moss
3 stems of pink celosia
10 stems of pink strawflowers
12 stems of pink globe amaranth
12 pods of love-in-a-mist
12 to 15 rosebuds
4 stems of white statice
1 head of hydrangea, broken into small segments
Medium-size rectangular basket, with handle
Hot glue gun and glue sticks, or thick white craft glue

WHAT YOU DO

1. Glue clumps of moss to the four corners of the basket rim and up one-third of the handle, as shown in the photo on the opposite page. Leave the rim bare in spots, to allow the color of the basket to peek through and become part of the decorative pattern.

2. Turning the basket as you work, glue on the largest flowers, like celosia, first; continue to add flowers of decreasing size. Trail some flowers down both the inside and outside of the basket—don't limit the material solely to the rim. Build up some of the material as you work, gluing some small flowers on top of larger ones to give a more three-dimensional effect. Cluster large flowers near the handle, where there's less chance of them getting broken off; use smaller flowers on the handle itself, decreasing flower size as you go up the handle.

Variations: If you plan to use this project to hold a plant, line the basket with heavy plastic or insert a saucer to catch the overflow from watering, then decorate as instructed above. If you like, you can create your own design, based on the materials you have available. You can decorate all around the rim or partway around the rim and up the handle.

Candle Bobeches

WHAT YOU NEED

6 tiny rosebuds
1 piece of foxtail
3 flower heads of globe amaranth
3 pods of love-in-a-mist
1 small sprig of German statice
1 Battenberg lace bobeche, to fit the candle
Hot or cool glue gun and glue sticks, or thick white craft glue
Flame retardant spray (optional)
1 candlestick
1 candle, to fit the candlestick

WHAT YOU DO

1. Glue the rosebuds in a small cluster on one outer edge of the bobeche.

2. Glue the remaining materials in a cluster from the inside of the bobeche out toward the edge.

3. If the lace bobeche is not pretreated, you may want to spray the finished project with flame retardant according to package directions. Even treated projects should be watched carefully when used with lit candles!

4. Place the bobeche on the candlestick and firmly insert the candle.

Variation: Make a miniature bouquet of flowers and grasses with stems about 3 inches long. The materials shown in the photo on the opposite page include foxtails, rosebuds, globe amaranths, and love-in-a-mist pods. Secure the bundle by wrapping it with floral wrapping tape in the middle. Tie a narrow wired ribbon bow under the lip of the candlestick. Use hot glue to attach the bouquet to the center of the bow, and arrange a loop of the bow to hide the tape on the bundle. You can place a plain lace bobeche under the candle for added decoration.

Branched Bower Wreath

The Branched Bower Wreath, based on a triangle of birch stems, is a wonderful way to bring the feeling of spring indoors. The fresh-picked stems are pliable, so it's easy to work them into the proper shape. Display the wreath on a door, or use it as a charming mantel decoration.

WHAT YOU NEED

About 12 fresh-cut stems of birch, each 3 to 4 feet long and of roughly pencil thickness

A few pieces of shelf fungus, bark, and green moss

1 to 2 handfuls of dried Spanish moss

3 stems each of globe thistle, statice, helipterum, bachelor's-button, winged everlasting, and pearly everlasting

6 feet of 22- or 24-gauge floral spool wire

Wire cutters

Hot glue gun and glue sticks, or thick white craft glue

Carved, ceramic, or other type of artificial bird and eggs

WHAT YOU DO

1. Soak the birch stems overnight in a bathtub if they've dried out too much to be pliable. If you use the branches within a few days after picking, you can omit this step.

2. Divide the stems into two piles of about six stems each. Lay the piles on a table with the cut ends facing each other, then overlap the cut ends by 1 foot. Think of keeping the finished base flat and wide. Rather than piling up all the stems to bind them together, spread each bundle out a bit. The base of the wreath should be about 3 inches deep, giving you a nice wide surface for attaching the decorative material.

3. With the wire, leave an end of 10 inches, and somewhat loosely bind the overlapped area from one side to the other. With wire cutters, cut the wire off the spool, leaving another end 10 inches long. Secure the wire at both ends by weaving it under and over several of the previous turns to hide it. Then cut off the excess wire and tuck the ends amid the stems.

Step 3

PROJECT POINTERS

Harvesting

Look for interesting bits of moss, fungus, or fallen bark around your home or on your walks or travels. You'll find natural riches in the most unlikely spots once you've trained your eyes for scouting. The best shelf fungus grows on old fallen wood. You might need a penknife to pry it off the log. When you get the fungus home, let it soak in hot soapy water for a few minutes, then leave it out on a rack to dry. Also treat fallen bark in this manner to rid it of any tiny creatures lurking between the layers.

Bachelor's-buttons (*Centaurea cyanus*) are a very easy annual to grow, and they sometimes reseed themselves. To retain the blue color, pick them for air drying the first day the flower opens; blue fades very quickly in older flowers.

4. Grasp the bud ends, one pile in each hand, about 6 inches from each end. Gently bring your hands together over the middle to form the top of the triangle. Cross the two bundles, with the stem tips splaying outward. Bind the two bundles together with wire, as you did in Step 3, at the point where they cross.

5. Glue the fungus onto the base of the wreath to broaden the "floor." Attach the bark and green moss with glue, along with some of the Spanish moss.

6. Make a nesting place for the bird and eggs with the rest of the Spanish moss; attach with glue. Glue the bird and eggs to the "nest."

7. Add the flowers, gluing them in a vertical position. Group like kinds together, as they might grow in nature.

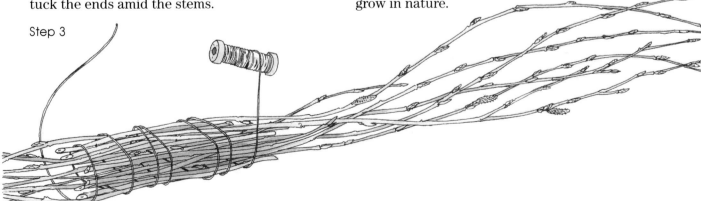

Hazel Spring Tree

One of my favorite plants for winter and early spring interest is contorted hazel (*Corylus avellana* 'Contorta'). Its twisted branches dip, swirl, and corkscrew. In spring, the catkins that formed the previous autumn become bright and pendulous. Bring a few of the branches indoors to create this dramatic spring "tree" for your living room.

WHAT YOU NEED

2 or 3 fresh or dried well-formed branches of contorted hazel, with catkins

Fresh or dried green moss

Small lichens or mushrooms

3 stems of pink larkspur (optional)

Medium-size clay or plastic flowerpot, to fit the jardiniere

Oriental-style jardiniere

Stones, foil, or cotton

Plaster of paris

Coffee can or other old container, for mixing the plaster

Disposable mixing stick

Hot glue gun and glue sticks, or thick white craft glue

WHAT YOU DO

1. Check to make sure that your flowerpot will fit inside the jardiniere without showing over the rim.

2. Plug up holes in the bottom of the flowerpot with the stones, foil, or cotton.

3. Have your branches ready; place them vertically in the pot to form a tree "trunk." See which way they will look best. When you are ready to embed them in the plaster, there's not much time to change their placement.

4. When you're satisfied with their placement, remove the branches. Mix the plaster of paris with the disposable stick according to package directions. Pour into the flowerpot within 1 inch of the rim.

5. While the plaster is wet, embed the branches in it in the arrangement you have chosen. You may have to hold the branches for a few minutes until the plaster hardens enough to support them.

6. When the plaster is hard (after about 5 minutes), place the pot in the jardiniere. Cover the plaster with the green moss, mounding it in some places to make it look more interesting. Glue on lichens or mushrooms.

7. If desired, remove individual flowers from the larkspur stems, and glue them in a random pattern to the tips of the branches, as if the tree were in spring bloom.

PROJECT POINTERS

Growing

Contorted hazel is also known as Harry Lauder's walking stick, after the twisted cane of a Scottish comedian. This plant will do well in either sun or partial shade, and grows slowly to about 7 feet. It's available from your local nursery or from the Wayside Gardens catalog (see Appendix D on page 154 for their address). You may have to wait a year after planting before the tree is large enough to prune.

Harvesting

Carefully examine the branches of your tree before you cut them, keeping in mind both the final shape of the tree and the shape of the branches you need for this project. Select branches that are well twisted, somewhat horizontal, and full of catkins. If you don't have access to a contorted hazel tree, substitute contorted willow or contorted mulberry. Your local florist should be able to provide you with these branches by special order.

As with most of my shrubs and trees, I postpone pruning the contorted hazel until I need some branches for a craft project or an arrangement. This way I usually have the material I need and the plant is kept under control.

When you harvest, always use sharp pruning shears to avoid crushing or tearing the remaining stems. As you prune, make the cut close to a main stem or branch so you don't leave a stub, which can be a good entry point for insects and disease organisms. Contorted hazels often produce straight, fast-growing suckers from their bases. Cut these straight shoots off just below the soil surface to keep them from ruining the plant's spreading form.

Drying

You can work with the branch as soon as you cut it, or let it air dry before you work with it. If fresh, it will dry naturally in the pot.

Flowered Swirl Wreath

For a wild, wide, and wonderful craft, try this Flowered Swirl Wreath. Place it on a large wall or in a stairwell where it can be displayed to best advantage. A light-colored background shows off the silhouette of each fine twig and bud. You can substitute dried flowers other than the ones listed here, if you prefer.

WHAT YOU NEED
(for a 38-inch-diameter wreath)

72 stems of birch, beech, or other similar wood,
    12 to 16 inches long with swelling buds
20 stems of sorghum
12 stems of fresh, branched boxwood leaves
20 stems of pink larkspur
12 stems of pink celosia
20 stems of peach strawflowers
12 red roses
8 inches of floral spool wire
Floral wrapping tape (optional)
Hillman wreath form, 12 inches in diameter
Pliers
Pruning shears
Hot glue gun and glue sticks, or thick white
    craft glue

WHAT YOU DO

1. Divide the branches into 12 piles of six stems each.

2. Using the wire and tape, if desired, make a wire hanger and attach it to the wreath form. See Appendix B on page 146 for instructions on making and attaching wire hangers.

3. Taking the wreath form, set the ends of one pile of branches in one of the wreath form's wire clamps. Use the pliers to bend the clamp wires over *tightly*, one side at a time, and squeeze very hard. This way the branches won't slip out as they continue to dry and shrink. However, you can easily reopen and close the wreath clamps to make any necessary adjustments.

4. Take the next pile of branches, and lay it in the clamp below the first pile, overlapping the first stem ends and the clamp with the buds of the second pile, and clamp in the same way as the first pile was done. Now squeeze this second clamp tightly, as in Step 3.

5. Continue around the wreath frame in this manner. When you get to the last pile, it will be a little harder as you try to hide the eleventh clamp and still tuck in the stems of the twelfth pile.

6. Hang the wreath from a hook or nail to finish the construction. If any stems stick out too far, clip them off at the stem end with pruning shears.

7. Insert one or two stems of sorghum in each clamp, pointing them in the same direction

as the branches. Make them a little shorter than the longest branches. You will have enough room to slip the sorghum in between the branches. Add the boxwood leaves, and tuck them in between the stems.

8. Next insert the larkspur in the same manner, one or two stems in each clamp, slightly shorter than the sorghum.

9. Next add the celosia and the strawflowers in the same manner. If you can no longer squeeze anything else within the confines of the clamps, glue the additional flowers onto the wreath. Add the roses last, as these are the most precious and you want them to be highly visible.

Step 3

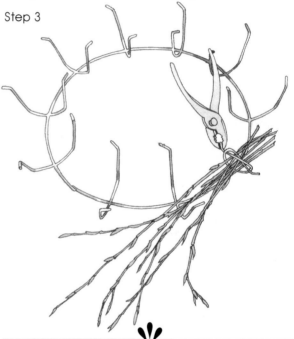

PROJECT POINTERS

Harvesting

Strawflower stems are somewhat fragile, hence the common practice of wiring strawflower heads. For this project, use wired strawflowers so you can turn the heads to face front in the finished wreath.

Drying

Boxwood is one of the few types of leaves that retain a good green color when dried, but it is also quite brittle to work with. So cut and use boxwood while it is still fresh and pliable, and for more graceful lines, allow it to dry in the arrangement.

Pussy Willow Swirl Wreath

Celebrate the arrival of the new growing season by forming this exuberant Pussy Willow Swirl Wreath. Although it may use the whole spring harvest of one shrub, the finished product is well worth it. Hang it in your home or workplace and enjoy the beauty for many years.

WHAT YOU NEED

60 stems of air-dried pussy willow, in full bud, 12 to 15 inches long
8 inches of thin wire
Floral wrapping tape (optional)
Hillman wreath form, 10 inches in diameter
Pliers (optional)
Pruning shears

WHAT YOU DO

1. Divide pussy willow branches into ten piles of six stems each.

2. Using the wire and tape, if desired, make a wire hanger and attach it to the wreath form. See Appendix B on page 146 for instructions on making and attaching wire hangers.

3. Taking the wreath form, set the ends of the first pile of pussy willows in a clamp with the branches at a slight angle. Bend the clamp over *tightly*, one side at a time; use the pliers, if desired, to squeeze very hard. This way the branches won't slip out as they continue to dry and shrink. However, you can easily reopen and close the wreath clamps to make any necessary adjustments.

4. Take the next pile of branches and lay it in the clamp below the first pile, overlapping the first stem ends and the first clamp, and tighten the second clamp in the same manner as the first was done. Now squeeze this second clamp tightly, as above.

Step 4

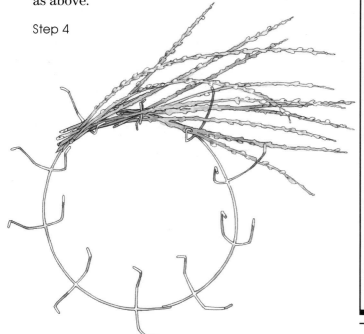

5. Continue around the wreath form in this manner. When you get to the last pile it will be a little harder as you try to hide the ninth clamp and still tuck in the stems of the tenth pile.

6. Check your wreath. If any stems stick out too far, clip them off at the stem end with pruning shears. If a bud end sticks out too far, gently push it toward the center of the wreath.

PROJECT POINTERS

Growing

Pussy willows are easy to grow from cuttings. When you get branches from a friend's garden or a flower shop, recut the stems and let them stand in water in a coffee can until first roots develop. Then each week add a cup or so of soil to the water, never letting this slurry dry out. Eventually you will have branches with good "soil roots," different from the glistening white "water roots" that developed first. Plant the rooted stems outdoors, one branch to a hole, leaving 10 or more feet between the new plants. Continue to water throughout the first spring and summer because willows like moisture for growth. They are extremely fast growing; from a 3-foot stem cutting you could easily have a 6-foot shrub within a year. Mature pussy willows are actually small trees, growing up to 25 feet high and 15 feet wide. To keep them under control, cut a few of the oldest stems down to the ground each year.

Harvesting

Pick branches when the buds have opened to the fat, silvery catkins. Be careful not to leave suitable branches on the plant too long; once the yellow pollen ripens, the catkins drop quickly and leaves appear.

Drying

Let the branches stand in a cardboard carton for about a week to air dry naturally before starting the project. Some desirable shrinkage will occur during that time, but the catkins will still be firmly attached. Use the branches for craft work within two weeks, or the branches will get too brittle for this project.

Peony Pockets and Rose Ring

Peonies and roses, two of the most fragrant garden flowers, are the components of these aromatic crafts. Display a Peony Pocket (*bottom*) on an end table, shelf, or dresser with a grouping of other collectibles. Or cluster several to highlight the unusual beauty of the dried peonies. The Rose Ring (*top*) looks equally delightful displayed on an interior wall or used as a door hanging.

Peony Pockets

WHAT YOU NEED (for 1 pocket)

5 or more air-dried peonies, with their leaves, on
     stems 10 to 15 inches long
4 stems of baby's-breath or white statice
Funnel or tapered bottle
Plastic wrap
Round cotton or linen doily, 8 to 12 inches in
     diameter
Fabric stiffener
2 feet of narrow satin ribbon
Scissors
Green floral wrapping tape

WHAT YOU DO

1. To make the form, cover the outside of a funnel or tapered bottle with plastic wrap.

2. To make the doily pocket, soak the clean doily in a mixture of 1 part water to 1 part fabric stiffener until saturated. Remove from the mixture and gently squeeze out excess liquid.

3. Drape the doily over and around the plastic-covered form. Smooth gently. Let dry in this shape for 12 to 24 hours.

4. When the doily is completely dry, slip out the form and any plastic wrap that adheres.

5. Weave a decorative narrow satin ribbon through the lace edge and make a bow.

6. Take the peonies in your hand one by one and make a small bouquet, with the center flow-ers higher than the outer ones. Fill in the bare spots with baby's-breath or statice.

7. Still holding the bouquet in one hand, wrap the stems together securely with the tape, stretching it as you go.

8. Place the bouquet in the doily holder. Cut the stems with scissors, if necessary, so the flowers will fit snugly into the doily. The flower bouquet should be about one-and-a-half times taller than the holder.

Variation: Use a tube or cylindrical bottle wrapped in plastic to make a peony pocket that is open at both ends. Follow Steps 2 through 5, weaving ribbon through both ends of the pocket. Make two bouquets of peonies as in Steps 6 and 7, using at least three peonies in each. Slip the bouquets into each end of the stiffened doily.

Step 4

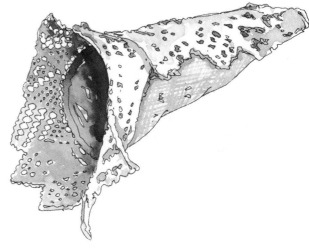

Step 3

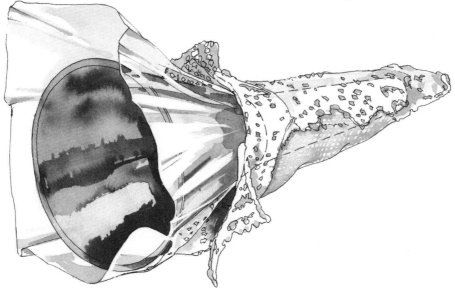

❧

PROJECT POINTERS

Growing

Peonies (*Paeonia* spp.) fall into one of two groups: the herbaceous ones, which die back every year, and the much more expensive tree peonies, which retain their woody forms throughout the year. Most peonies are adapted to grow in Zones 3 to 8, although hardiness varies among species and cultivars. If you enjoy peonies as much for their scent as for their flower forms, be aware that some cultivars have no fragrance. Either take a test sniff before you buy, or look for catalog descriptions that mention the scent.

When planting, place tree peonies at the same depth at which they grew in the nursery. Plant the crowns of herbaceous peonies so the eyes (buds) are 1 to 2 inches below the soil surface. Herbaceous peonies sometimes fail to bloom, and deep planting is a common cause. If you suspect this is a problem, dig up the plants and replace them at the proper level.

Drying

When you dry peonies, some faint aroma remains, which adds to the enjoyment of working with them. There are two ways to dry peonies: air drying and processing in silica gel. For a massive formal presentation, I prefer the individual perfection of those dried in silica gel. For an informal bunched look, the air-dried peonies have a wonderful old-fashioned quality.

Light-pink, deep-pink, or wine-colored peonies look best after drying; white flowers turn beige. Pick flowers before they are fully opened but after the petals have all hatched from the buds. Without removing the leaves, hang in a warm, dry, dark spot for about two weeks to dry.

Shrub rose flower clusters can be air dried easily in about five days on a cookie rack in a warm, dry, dark spot.

Floribundas, grandifloras, and hybrid tea roses can be air dried by clustering the stems in a rubber band and hanging them upside down for about two weeks.

Rose Ring

WHAT YOU NEED (for a 9-inch ring)

1 fresh cane of a double-flowered pink shrub rose in bloom, at least 3 feet long
10 small air-dried flower clusters from another part of the pink shrub rose
3 large air-dried rose flowers, such as 'Peace' or 'Tropicana'
22- or 24-gauge floral spool wire
Thick gardening gloves
Wire cutters
Hot glue gun and glue sticks, or thick white craft glue

WHAT YOU DO

1. Have the wire handy. Don your gloves. Hold the long rose cane at one end with one hand. With your other hand, bend the cane into a small circle, 9 to 12 inches in diameter, and weave the excess length in and out along the circle. You will have a small wreath that holds by itself, with rose clusters sticking out in odd directions.

2. Tie the wire to the rose cane anywhere along the wreath. Now, moving clockwise, wrap the wire around the wreath, grasping the little clusters of blooms and turning them to the front or top of the wreath wherever possible. The flowers will now be tamed and orderly.

3. When you have gone completely around the ring, cut the wire, leaving a 6-inch end, and tie it off on the back, leaving a little loop for hanging.

4. Hang the ring in a warm, dark, dry place for about two weeks to dry completely. Turn it every few days so it will dry evenly and not droop or sag. When the ring is dry, there will probably be some uneven spots. Add the extra dried rose clusters where needed to fill in where the blooms are sparse. Glue in place.

5. Glue on the large roses for accent, either in a cluster at the top of the wreath, or at two, six, and ten o'clock around the ring.

Variations: Other flowers and plant materials can also be used as accents on your rose ring. Tuck some sprigs of baby's-breath or eucalyptus into the ring, placing them evenly around the wreath or clustering them around the large roses.

Step 2

PROJECT POINTERS

Growing

I succumbed to the zealous prose of the catalog writers and ordered my first shrub roses several years ago. After the first year, the shrubs took off and now look even better than the color photographs. As advertised, all of this beauty takes little work—no spraying, no pruning, just feeding and picking off a few Japanese beetles in the summer. By the third year, the bloom was so prolific that I sacrificed some of the excess to craft projects. From three shrubs, I made five rose rings and cut 2 pounds of (dried) rosebuds and a full tray of flower clusters. I never even noticed

a change in the appearance of the shrubs. If you have a little extra room in your garden, I suggest you try at least one of these wonderful plants.

Harvesting

Cut the long rose cane when about one-third of the blossoms are completely open, but two-thirds are still in quarter or half bud. If you pick too early, you won't get enough color in the ring. If you pick too late and most of the flowers are opened, many will shatter during the process of forming the wreath.

Work with the cane as soon as you pick it, so it will be pliable.

Lavender Triangle and Pussy Willow Heart

Both lavender and pussy willow have great sensuous appeal. The heady perfume of lavender and the velvety sheen and softness of pussy willow lend themselves to many romantic projects. If you can bear to hide it away from view, hang the Lavender Triangle (*bottom*) inside your linen or clothes closet door to capture the fragrance. The Pussy Willow Heart (*top*) is a perfect decoration for a wall or door.

Lavender Triangle

WHAT YOU NEED

3 bunches of lavender, each about 15 inches long
3 roses, with leaves, stems cut to 1 inch
2 tiny pressed pansies
Brown or green floral wrapping tape
Hot glue gun and glue sticks, or thick white craft glue
3 yards of ribbon, cut into three 1-yard pieces

WHAT YOU DO

1. Divide one bunch of lavender into two equal parts. Turn one part end over end and place it next to the stems of the other part, so the flowers of one part are on top of the stem ends of the other part. You'll have a wand of lavender with flowers at each end.

2. Use the tape to bind the stems together near each end, 1 inch below the flowers. Stretch the tape gently as you work with it, and it will stick to itself as you wrap.

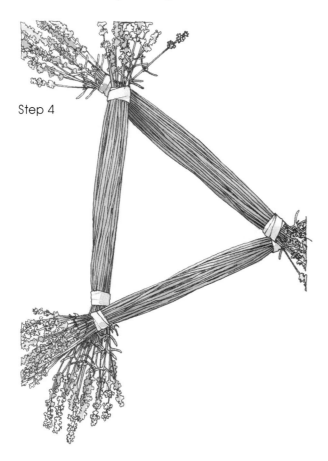

Step 4

3. Repeat Steps 1 and 2 with the other two bunches of lavender. Now you'll have three secure wands, one for each side of the triangle.

4. Lay the three wands (Sides 1, 2, and 3) on your work table in a triangular pattern. Lay the taped area at one end of Side 1 across a taped area on Side 2 to form an X. Secure the two wands with a large dab of glue. After the glue dries, lay the other end of Side 2 across one end of Side 3, forming another X, and attach them with glue. Allow glue to dry. Finally, lay the free end of Side 3 over the free end of Side 1, and glue them together.

5. Tie a ribbon bow at each intersection to hide the tape and glue.

6. Tuck in any stray stems, then glue one rose to the center of each bow. Glue one pansy on either side of the top rose.

PROJECT POINTERS

Growing

Hardy lavenders, such as *Lavandula angustifolia,* are easy perennials to grow in full sun and well-drained soil. The gray-green leaves make a pleasant addition to the garden both before and after the flowers bloom. There are many lavender species and cultivars, all of which are suitable for this project. My favorite is *Lavandula × intermedia* 'Grosso', which has wonderfully long flower spikes.

Harvesting

In the morning after the dew has evaporated, pick lavender for drying. Pick long stems on which the blooms have just started to open, well before any trace of brown shows in the flowers. Don't worry if the stems are shorter than 15 inches; you can still use them to make a smaller, daintier triangle. If you keep harvesting the first crop of flowers, the plants will often produce a second flush of blooms in the fall.

Although this project uses only stems and flowers, save the leaves for drying. I usually include some leaves in my potpourri; they are strongly scented and of a pleasing gray color.

Lavender

Pussy Willow Heart

WHAT YOU NEED

8 stems of fresh-cut pussy willow, each about 3 feet long
7 roses, with leaves (optional)
Several pressed fern fronds (optional)
Floral spool wire
Wire cutters
3 yards of wired ribbon
6 inches of thin wire
Hot glue gun and glue sticks, or thick white craft glue

WHAT YOU DO

1. Divide the pussy willow into two piles of four stems each. Bind the stems of one pile securely with the floral spool wire 2 inches from the bottom. Cut the wire.

2. Repeat with the other pile.

3. Place the piles in front of you on the table, bud ends pointing away from you. Overlap the ends of the two piles at the site of the wires, forming a V.

4. Bind the two piles together securely, maintaining the V shape. To bind, wrap the floral spool wire tightly around all the stems, and also through the V several times, then around all the stems again. Cut with the wire cutters and twist the cut end in and out through the stems so it won't unwrap.

5. Grasp the bud ends of each pile together and bind all the stems with the floral spool wire about 8 inches from the tips. Don't cut the wire. Pull the wire gently to the base of the V. The heart shape will gradually form as you pull down the buds to meet the stem ends. At the place where the wire wrapping at the tips meets the wire wrapping at the ends, wrap the heart tightly with the floral spool wire.

6. Make a bow with the ribbon and the thin wire, leaving one end with a 15-inch tail. See Appendix A on page 144 for complete bow-making instructions. Glue or wire the bow to the top of the heart where the pussy willow stems cross.

7. If desired, you can use roses and ferns to decorate the heart. Glue the ferns to the willow stems. Cut the rose stems short, and glue each flower individually to the wreath as desired. Glue the rose leaves on as well for additional color and interest. If your dried roses have shrunk too badly or if your purchased dried rosebuds are too misshapen and compressed, steam them opened gently by holding each over the spout of a boiling teakettle for about 1 minute and gently opening the flower by hand. Don't overdo this process, because excess humidity can fade flower color.

Pussy willows

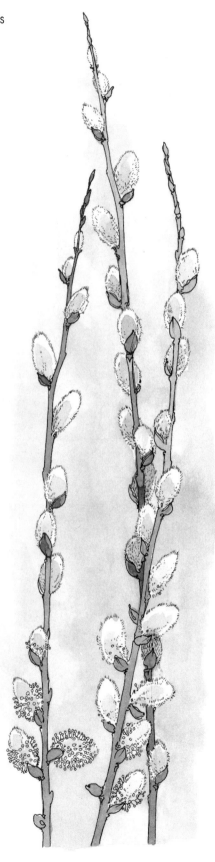

Step 5

PROJECT POINTERS

Harvesting

Use only fresh pussy willow for the heart project. Dried stems will be too brittle to bend. See "Project Pointers" on page 55 for further information on planting and harvesting.

If you want to make this heart for Valentine's Day, you can cut the pussy willow in early January and force it into bud indoors. Cut the branches in January or February and let them stand indoors in clean water out of direct sunlight.

THE SUMMER GARDEN

For me, summer begins once spring planting is over. I've sown the remaining seeds, transplanted the last seedling into the garden, and planted the cover crop. The windowsills in my farmhouse, minus their seed flats, are back to normal with vases and pottery and candlesticks. I'll have some additional planting later in the summer—another crop of glads, some biennials like honesty and caraway, a late planting of larkspur for next year's bloom, fall bulbs—but for now, I feel the satisfaction of a major task completed.

Even before scattering the last seed, I harvest the first crop for drying. Chive flowers are followed quickly by chamomile, peonies, and lamb's-ears. As the summer starts, the roses are ripe for snipping, and the globe centaureas and globe thistles are showing color. Many of the shrubs I planted several years ago are finally big enough to cut. The 'Nikko Blue' hydrangea I put in four years ago is blooming for the first time this year. I'll make a note to remind myself to cut the flowers for drying later in the season. The shrub rose 'Ferdy' is a riot of coral its third season at the Meadow Lark; three bushes provide me with tons of rose buds, blooms, and branches for drying.

As the summer progresses, I notice that some plantings are tall and full, while others are weak and spindly. Some seeds that I culled from last year's crop, like the cleome and cockscomb, usually germinate and grow well. But I'm not always so lucky with my other experiments. One year I direct-sowed *Nigella orientalis* seeds that I collected from some purchased seedpods. Unfortunately, they were not viable, and they left 6 feet of empty space in my row. Next time I'll test unfamiliar seeds by starting a few indoors before wasting precious garden space.

Weeding the garden always seems like a never-ending battle. The combination of raised beds, intensive planting, and plowing or mulching between the rows cuts down on the weeding time once the flowers have grown tall enough to shade the beds. In early summer, though, I take great care to weed regularly. The famous baseball player Satchel Paige must have been a gardener as well as a pitcher—his admonition "Don't look back: Something might be gaining on you" certainly applies to weeds! I barely get finished before it's time to start weeding all over again. Luckily, this only lasts a few weeks, until the plants are well established and I can cover the ground with mulch to keep the weeds under control.

Summer often finds me searching in vain for signs of rain. I listen to erratic weather predictions hoping for a favorable report, and dream about day-long summer showers. My automatic sprinkling system is more unreliable than the weather reports, working about 50 percent of the time and not reaching every crop even when fully operational. Mulching helps to conserve moisture, but sometimes it's not enough. I tell myself that what you can't control, you must let go, but it pains me to see a lush crop wither and brown in the summer drought. One consolation is that a drought season makes for excellent drying conditions. Perennials that prefer less water, like German statice, sea hollies, and gray-leaved artemisias, dry quickly in the barn once cut.

Each year I experiment with growing and drying new plant materials. This year perhaps I'll try burying bright, plump strawberries in silica gel, and maybe set some hard red crab apples near my furnace to see how they dry. I always choose my best available conditions for test-drying. If I don't like the results under those conditions, then I know the experiment was a failure. If the results are favorable, I make a note of my success for future reference.

Culinary Herb Wreath and Zinnias in a French Style

In many homes, the kitchen is the center of activity, so don't neglect this room as an important site for decoration. Hang the Culinary Herb Wreath (*left*) near your work area to enjoy the wonderful fragrance. Arranged in a shallow saucepan, fresh Zinnias in a French Style (*right*) are appropriate for a kitchen counter, breakfast room table, or picnic table.

Culinary Herb Wreath

WHAT YOU NEED

About 240 stems of fresh culinary herbs, each
6 inches long

Additional herbs, spices, or dried edibles for
decoration, such as hot red or green peppers,
garlic heads, cinnamon sticks, rose hips,
staghorn sumac, pepperberries, okra pods,
or dried beans

22- or 24-gauge floral spool wire

Brown floral wrapping tape

Wire cutters

Pruning shears or scissors

Flat wire wreath frame, 14 inches in diameter

4-inch floral picks

WHAT YOU DO

1. Before you bunch the herbs, pick over
them carefully and remove any yellow or damaged leaves. Then make 30 bunches of eight stems
per bunch, and secure each with a rubber band.
Bunch the herbs so the topmost leaves or flowers
are even, then trim the bottom ends of the stems
even, too.

2. Using an 8-inch piece of the wire and the
tape, if desired, make a wire hanger and attach it
to the wreath frame. See Appendix B on page 146
for instructions on making and attaching wire
hangers.

3. Tie the end of the spool of wire to the
wreath frame.

4. Decide on a design scheme. Put the wreath
frame flat on the work table. Lay the first three
bunches of herbs on the frame and wrap very
tightly with the wire.

5. Lay the next three bunches on top of the
stems of the first three, hiding the rubber bands
and frame, and wrap with the wire.

6. Continue placing and wrapping the herb
bunches, overlapping the stems until you have
covered the wreath frame.

7. Cut off the wire, leaving about 6 inches.
Tie this end tightly to the back of the wreath to
secure the herbs.

8. To dry the wreath, hang from a nail in a
warm, dry, dark place. The herbs will droop as
they dry. Each day you *must* rotate this wreath
one-quarter turn until it is fully dried, so that all
of the herbs will dry straight and even.

9. To decorate the wreath with additional
herbs, spices, or dried edibles, wrap a stem or
group of stems with the wire of a floral pick.
Cover the wire with the tape. Stick the pick down
through the herbs and under a piece of wire
frame to secure it.

Step 4

PROJECT POINTERS

Growing

People are sometimes concerned about
bringing bugs into the house on fresh herbs
and flowers. My advice is not to worry about
it too much. There's really no way to be sure
that your plant materials are insect-free, but
there are some things you can do to minimize the chances of bringing in bugs. Check
your plants regularly during the growing
season, and control pests before they get
out of hand. As you harvest, look at the leaves,
stems, and flowers carefully. If you see a few
insects, handpick or wash them off with a
spray of water. And if the plants are too buggy,
just don't pick from them!

❧

PROJECT POINTERS

Harvesting

Don't be put off by the number of stems used for this project—this is only an approximate number. When you look around your garden, you'll probably find all the materials you need. Even a small plant can produce a surprising number of stems. One handful of parsley, for example, may have 20 to 30 stems. If your herbs are bushy, you can use less; if you harvest them with long stems, you may be able to cut them into several pieces. It all adds up very quickly. If your harvest is not abundant, make a smaller wreath.

Drying

Select herbs for the wreath with an eye to color, texture, and shape. Look for herbs in flower, like marjoram, mint, or basil, and in the seed stage, like dill or caraway. Look for contrasts in the color of leaves, such as purple basil and gray-green sage. The color of the fresh leaf is not a good indication of the color when dried. Many of the bright-green herbs turn brown when dried, rather than staying green. Parsley, bay, green santolina, and most mints maintain their green color well for more than a year.

Many of the most delicious culinary herbs are quite fragile when dried, and crumble readily during wreathmaking. You can avoid this problem by assembling the wreath when the herbs are fresh-cut and by allowing the whole wreath to dry. Keep in mind that in the process the herbs will lose one-third to one-half of their volume. Because of this natural shrinkage, the fresh wreath must look overabundant. Then, after the drying, it will still look full but not overdone, as you can see in the photo of the dried Culinary Herb Wreath on page 66. If you find some sparse patches after drying is complete, you can always tuck in a few extra herbs to cover the spot.

Zinnias in a French Style

WHAT YOU NEED

11 fresh-cut large zinnias, like the 'Zenith' hybrids, in an assortment of pink, peach, and red tones, with stems at least 12 inches long
14 fresh-cut medium-size zinnias, like 'Border Beauty Rose', in an assortment of pink, peach, and red tones, with stems at least 6 inches long
14 fresh-cut rigid leaves, like rhododendron, viburnum, or iris
Large handful of fresh or dried Spanish moss
Pruning shears
2 buckets full of water
Cut-flower food (optional)
2 bricks of green floral foam
Paring knife
Large, shallow pan or other container

WHAT YOU DO

1. Cut the large and medium-size zinnias and the leaves in early morning or early evening for best longevity. By hand, strip off all leaves from the zinnias and plunge the stems into one bucket of water almost to their heads. Bundle the rigid leaves in a rubber band and stand them in the water with the zinnias. If you have cut-flower food, add it to the bucket according to package directions, if desired. Let stand for at least 3 hours or overnight. This process, called conditioning of fresh-cut flowers and leaves, is essential before arranging them in foam.

2. Add cut-flower food, if desired, to the second bucket of water. Soak the two bricks of floral foam for 30 minutes.

3. Now cut the wet bricks of foam with the paring knife so they will completely pave the bottom of the container, coming out to the edges. For a round container, cut the bricks in half the long way first, then fit the foam in one side. Keep cutting and adding other pieces until the surface of the container is filled to the edges. It doesn't need to look neat and even—just be sure it's tightly wedged in all around.

4. Spread the Spanish moss out over the foam to hide it from view.

5. Cut all the large zinnia stems to 12 inches. Cut all the medium-size zinnias to 6 inches.

6. Insert the stems into the wet foam, starting in the center with a large zinnia, then make two rings of large flowers around the center one, and another outer ring of medium-size zinnias. Take care to place the flowers so they are as level and as even as possible. Turn the arrangement as you work. Check on the straightness of the stems and the evenness of the top.

7. Finish off the arrangement with a circle of rigid leaves around the rim. Insert the stems in the foam, between the zinnias. Try to get the tips of the leaves level.

8. Add water to the pan to cover the foam, and add water daily to keep the arrangement in peak condition.

Step 6

PROJECT POINTERS

Design

When I need a container for a flower arrangement, I like to look beyond the standard vase or basket to the unusual containers that are lurking on shelves in every room of the house. For dried flowers, the choices are endless. Since the container doesn't need to hold water, anything from an old cowboy boot or a child's dollhouse to a hat turned upside down can inspire you to produce an interesting arrangement.

For fresh flowers, look for any watertight container or one that can accept a plastic liner to hold wet floral foam. (Flowers last longer in plain water, but many times you'll find that floral foam will give you better control in placing the flowers and thus help you create the special effect you're looking for.) Search your kitchen cabinets for common objects that make uncommon flower containers. Coffeemakers, food processors, pots, and pans can all hold water and create surprising and amusing containers.

Growing

Zinnias are among the easiest annuals to grow from seed. Sow directly in the garden following package directions, or start indoors in late spring for earlier bloom. Select a cultivar that grows at least 20 inches tall to use in flower arranging. Save the lilliputians for the front of the border.

Harvesting

Frequent cuttings increase the abundance of zinnias, so don't hesitate to strip the garden; more flowers will be awaiting you next week.

A Salute to the Flag

Here's a different way to celebrate a holiday—
use dried flowers to pave the surface of an old wooden
flat in a flag pattern. Display the flag as a centerpiece
to commemorate an occasion with a patriotic theme,
or stand it on an upturned wooden crate tilting against
the house to welcome guests at the front porch.

WHAT YOU NEED

1-gallon bag of sphagnum moss
Large handful of Spanish moss
20 heads of globe thistle with stems at least 3 inches long
12 to 15 large heads of deep red cockscomb with stems at least 3 inches long
3 bunches of pearly everlasting with stems at least 3 inches long
Old wooden planting flat, tomato case, or low box (about 17 inches × 14 inches)
4 bricks of green or soft brown floral foam
Scissors or pruning shears
Small knife
Hot glue gun and glue sticks, or thick white craft glue

WHAT YOU DO

1. Line the inside of the wooden container with bricks of floral foam. The foam must come all the way to the edges. You can cut up small pieces to stuff into any empty corners. This job doesn't need to look neat—it won't show.

2. Tuck bits of sphagnum moss between the foam and the edges of the flat.

3. Strew the Spanish moss over the "star" section of the flag, the upper lefthand corner, in an area about 6 inches × 7 inches. This prevents the foam from peeking out after the project is completed.

4. Cut the stems of the globe thistle to 3 inches long. Insert in rows in the upper lefthand corner of the flat. Here I have five stars across and four stars down. Keep the rows even and the tops of the globe thistle level with each other.

5. In this flat there are five stripes, each about 2½ inches wide. Start with the top stripe of cockscomb. Break up flower heads if they are too big. Save the pieces to glue in the spaces to make an even row. Stick flower stems into the foam, trying to keep the row even.

6. Cut the stems of the pearly everlasting to about 3 inches. Insert the stems into the foam one by one, keeping the edges of the stripe even and the tops of the flowers as level as possible.

7. Continue alternating red and white stripes.

8. If your wooden container has cut-out handles and slats as mine does, tuck in bits of sphagnum moss to hide the foam inside.

9. Make final adjustments to the flowers by gluing in any extra bits needed to even out the rows, but remember you are trying for overall effect, not close-up perfection. The flowers will never have that perfect, painted look, nor do you want them to.

Step 2

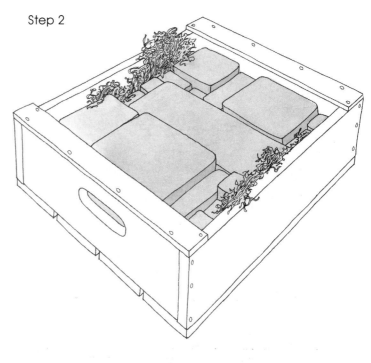

PROJECT POINTERS

Harvesting

Harvest globe thistle for drying when the color on the top of the ball becomes a dense blue but before the petals start to break out. The only way to tell the right time is to watch each day as the plant matures. Once you've picked some too early or too late, you will develop an eye for the right color. The center flower matures first, so cut it with a short stem to allow the others on the plant to ripen.

Pick pearly everlasting while it is still in bud—it will continue to open even after hung to dry. If you pick it when it is fully opened, you will have a mass of beautiful white fluff flying around as the seeds are released.

❧

Dried Flowers in a French Style

I first noticed this style of flower arranging on a trip to Paris. The densely packed, parallel stems make these arrangements strikingly different from the casual, country style. Try it yourself, using whatever straight-stemmed dried flowers you have in abundance. The finished arrangement makes a perfect complement to contemporary decor or provides a striking contrast in a more traditional setting.

WHAT YOU NEED

Large handful of Spanish moss or green sheet moss
24 to 36 or more stems of globe centaurea
Basket with straight sides, about 5 inches high and 11 inches long, with or without a handle
2 bricks of brown floral foam
Sharp knife
Pruning shears
3 strands of raffia

WHAT YOU DO

1. Pave the bottom of the basket with bricks of floral foam. With the knife, cut the foam as necessary to cover the bottom completely.

2. Cram the bricks of foam into the basket so there are no empty spaces and the bricks won't slide around. It's not very important for these bricks to be exactly even in height, but they must fit together tightly. Add slivers of foam at the edges to fill all the cracks.

3. Cover the foam with moss.

4. Decide what height you want your flowers to be. With the pruning shears, cut all the stem ends to the same length. If you cut the stem ends on a sharp angle, they are easy to insert into the foam.

5. If you are using a rectangular basket, start at the back of the basket and insert the stems into the foam in an even row. If you are using a round basket, start with the middle row. Push the stems into the foam so the flowers are standing perfectly straight and the heights of the flowers are even. The flower heads should be almost touching. The arrangement looks easy to duplicate, but the stems often don't want to behave. Don't be afraid to remove a flower and reinsert it if you're not satisfied at first, but keep in mind that the foam will start to deteriorate with too much rearranging.

6. Continue inserting flowers row after row until the basket is filled.

7. When the arrangement is complete, wrap the raffia around the stems, near the top, and tie a simple bow.

Variations: If you don't have globe centaurea, you can create a similar look with other materials. Use all one kind of any dried flower with strong stems at least 1 foot long. Instead of using just one kind of flower, you can also mix several types. For the project on the left in the photo on the opposite page, I combined larkspur, salal leaves, roses, poppy seedpods, and wire-stemmed white strawflowers in blocks of color. Within each block, the flowers are even on the sides and level on the top, but the heights of the blocks vary. The pointy tips of the salal leaves break the angularity of the flower blocks.

Follow the directions above, starting in the back of the basket. Complete one block of flowers at a time, ending with the shortest in front. Keep strawflowers low so the wire stems aren't visible. Experiment with the types of dried flowers, leaves, and stems you have in abundance. Try pussy willows, globe thistles, cockscombs, lavenders, peonies, sensitive fern, or grains like wheat, barley, and sorghum.

PROJECT POINTERS

Design

In this project and others, I have specified the quantities of plant materials so your finished projects can look like the ones shown in the photographs. But I wouldn't want you not to make a project just because you don't have the exact number of stems or flowers. In most cases, the quantities are quite flexible. There are always variations when you work with natural materials; stems can be shorter or longer, thinner or bushier. Some years you may have an abundance; in lean years, you may have to stretch things out. Please don't be stumped if you don't have the exact number or even the same flower. You can often substitute the flower that I recommend for another that you have. Or decide at the start to scale down (or up) the size of the project to fit your space and materials. Use your own common sense and creativity to adapt my ideas to your circumstances.

Harvesting

Pick globe centaurea (*Centaurea macrocephala*) when the gold color is just starting to show through the scaly pineapple-shaped calyx. The flowers will continue to ripen even after hanging to dry.

Insect Repellent Swag

Don't subject yourself and your stored clothes to the unpleasant odor of mothballs—protect your clothes with herbs instead! Create an Insect Repellent Swag from a variety of garden herbs, including wormwood, southernwood, yarrow, pennyroyal, tansy, lavender, and sage. Any lingering aroma on clothes or blankets is mild and pleasing to the nostrils, reminiscent of the summer harvest.

WHAT YOU NEED

1 small bunch each of wormwood, southernwood,
    yarrow, pennyroyal, tansy, lavender, and
    sage
6 stems of cockscomb (optional)
Pruning shears or heavy-duty scissors
2 strong rubber bands
1½ yards of natural-color twisted paper ribbon
Scissors

PROJECT POINTERS

Growing

Tansy is a wonderful perennial for late-summer color, but it spreads rampantly. Keep it in check in your garden by pulling out unwanted roots.

WHAT YOU DO

1. Lay out the bunches of herbs on your work table. Take off any ties or binding they might have.

2. The finished swag will be flat-backed to hang against a door or wall. Start with the wormwood. Lay that down first, then the southernwood next to it, but with the tips slightly lower. Put the yarrow on top of the wormwood, but again a bit lower.

3. Continue adding groups of the herbs and the cockscomb, if desired, ending with the sage.

4. Grasp the entire swag in one hand. Trim the stems evenly on the bottom, using the shears or scissors.

5. Still holding the swag, wrap the bottom tightly in a rubber band. Add the second rubber band over the first for added security.

6. Since the finished swag will hang upside down, place it that way on the work table. Untwist the paper ribbon, and wrap it around the stems, hiding the rubber bands. Tie it tightly in a knot, then make a bow. Using scissors, trim off any excess ribbon.

Step 2

Lilies under Glass

Dried lilies? Dried irises? These flowers will not dry well just by hanging, but with silica gel, all things are possible. To highlight the form of the individual flowers, arrange them in a simple, oriental style, using a few mature blossoms along with buds and leaves. This distinctive style is particularly attractive with contemporary decor.

WHAT YOU NEED

Clump moss
2 seedpods of yellow flag iris
2 rubrum lilies
3 buds of Dutch iris
3 leaves of Dutch iris
Small piece of floral clay
Small metal pinholder
**Wood base with new or antique glass display
    dome**
Smooth white river stones
Scissors or pruning shears
**Hot glue gun and glue sticks, or thick white craft
    glue**

Step 2

WHAT YOU DO

1. Press the clay on the bottom of the metal pinholder. Position the pinholder slightly off-center of the wood base and press down firmly.

2. Cover the pinholder with moss, so no metal shows. Secure the moss by pushing it down slightly over the pinholder.

3. Insert the tallest iris seedpod into the pinholder, checking to see that it clears the height of the dome when closed. The stem should lean slightly to the left front. Insert the shorter iris seedpod next to the first one at a similar angle. You may need to trim the stems with scissors or pruning shears to make them a suitable length.

4. Glue one of the lilies about one-third of the way down the stem of the shorter seedpod. The flower should point slightly upward and out.

5. Glue the other lily to the moss base, tilting the bloom slightly to one side.

6. Add the Dutch iris buds and leaves one at a time, filling in the space to give a three-dimensional look. Be sure to insert the stems firmly into the pinholder to secure them. If necessary, wedge in other little pieces of stem to tighten the arrangement.

7. Place several white river stones at the base of the composition to add a peaceful note. You may glue these in place so they don't move when you dust the dome.

PROJECT POINTERS

Drying

For drying in silica gel, follow the package directions. I always wear a face mask or respirator when working with silica gel, to avoid breathing in the powdery dust. Make sure that your flowers are very fresh and free of surface moisture when you bury them in the gel.

Store the dried flowers in an airtight container until you are ready to use them. Choose a dry day for arranging your silica-dried flowers. Displayed under a glass dome, the flowers are safeguarded from moisture in the air and may last for years.

Plate Rings

Few things enhance a meal more than a beautifully set table. These Plate Rings are a welcome substitute for a standard table centerpiece—they are slim and delicate and sized to serve as a base for each dinner plate. When a hand brushes against the fresh herbs, they release a delightfully pungent aroma.

WHAT YOU NEED

Many small specimens of blossoms, leaves, moss, and pods
2 screw eyes
Picture hanging wire
Old printer's drawer
Hot glue gun and glue sticks

WHAT YOU DO

1. Affix the screw eyes and wire to the back of the drawer so you will be able to hang the finished sampler from any picture hook.

2. Plan the arrangement of your flowers. For this project I selected flowers from the brightest and finest of my air-dried materials and arranged them by color, ranging from white and pale yellow through purple and brown. You could try other themes, like a sampler from a favorite vacation spot, including twigs, pods, and grasses, or a collection of pressed materials.

3. Put the materials in their approximate places and move them around until you are satisfied. Glue each piece in place. If you're not planning to cover the finished tray with glass (which you can do to increase the longevity of the flowers), strive for a three-dimensional effect. Allow some of the flowers to burst out slightly from their compartments and the petals to overlap the next unit. Glue other flowers back flat against the wall. Leave about one-fifth of the compartments empty to accent the flower samples.

PROJECT POINTERS

Design

A summer sampler is a great way to use up odds and ends like stemless or short-stemmed flowers. Below is a list of the materials I used for this sampler, starting in the left column of the printer's drawer (see the photo on the opposite page):

Larkspur, strawflowers
Honesty pod, strawflowers, German statice
Honesty pod, annual statice, strawflower, *Helipterum humboldtianum*
Honesty pod, orange globe amaranth, globe centaurea, safflowers
Honesty pod, heliopsis
Honesty pod, gloriosa daisies, strawflowers, heliopsis
Calendula, pearly everlasting
Cockscomb, tansy/larkspur, rosebuds
Strawflower, helipterum, barley, green Japanese lanterns, helipterum
Yarrow, love-in-a-mist pods, moss, bells-of-Ireland
Cockscomb, rose, peony, globe amaranth
Bachelor's-button, rat-tail statice
Strawflowers, dahlias, globe thistles, poppy pod
Annual statice, honesty pods, strawflowers, annual statice
Larkspur (purple and blue)
Sensitive fern, lamb's-ears

To impart a slightly different look to the project, use different quantities of materials. Either fill the compartments completely, or just include a few choice specimens. Use some flower heads and some flowers on short stems. Make tiny bouquets with some flowers and tie them with small bits of raffia; tuck them into the long, narrow spaces. You can use lots of different colors, as I did here, or personalize your sampler to fit the color scheme of a room.

Summer Shade Garden Centerpiece

In the sweltering days of August, a fresh center-piece of foliage and flowers in greens and creams can add a cooling touch. Because the arrangement is really in two separate halves, you can move each piece separately and then re-form the S shape by pushing the two halves close together. You may want to then add a leaf or two to the side of the foam to hide any seam that shows.

WHAT YOU NEED

Assortment of fresh-cut foliage and green flowers
Cut-flower food (optional)
Floral foam ring (comes with a plastic bottom),
    12 inches in diameter
Sharp knife
2 buckets full of water
Dish towel

WHAT YOU DO

1. Plunge the fresh-cut foliage and flowers into a bucket of tepid water. If you are using the cut-flower food, dissolve according to package directions and add to the bucket. Let stand in a cool, dim place for at least 3 hours to condition the plant material.

2. When you are ready to arrange the flowers and leaves, cut the floral foam ring in half with the sharp knife. Soak the halves in the second bucket of water with cut-flower food, if using, for about 20 minutes, until thoroughly saturated.

3. Remove the halves of the ring from the bucket and let drain for 5 minutes. Wipe the bottoms carefully with a dish towel.

4. When you put the two parts of the ring together in a line facing in opposite directions you will have the S shape for the arrangement. Position the halves so that they are as close to each other as possible.

5. Start inserting the leaves horizontally at the base of the foam, building up layers of leaves, all parallel with the table. Work on one section at a time, going around the sides. As you go around the S, change the kind of leaf you are working with, but keep each kind in its own area.

6. Keep building up the sides until you reach the top surface. Slant your insertions then, to follow the curve of the foam.

7. On the top of the centerpiece, stand the leaves and flowers upright. Vary the heights of the different sections so they will look more interesting.

8. Keep working around the S, inserting the material in clusters, hiding all the foam. When you think you are finished, check for bare spots, and fill in with extra leaves and flowers.

9. This will be a long-lasting arrangement if you continue to water it. The easiest way is to carry the two halves back to the sink and submerge the foam in shallow water until it is resaturated, about 10 minutes. Let drain and wipe the bottom carefully before replacing on the table.

Step 7

PROJECT POINTERS

Harvesting

For this centerpiece I used zebra grass, bells-of-Ireland, blue spruce, lady's-mantle, 'Palace Purple' heuchera, 'Lime Green' flowering tobacco, variegated Solomon's seal, 'Green Envy' zinnias, pokeweed, variegated false dragon head, Japanese holly, variegated Japanese pieris, white pine, mountain mint, and Scotch broom. These are not all shade plants; in fact, many crave sun. But the result is a centerpiece that looks shady and cool.

Spiral Tree Topiary

A Spiral Tree Topiary is a wonderful way to use up any flower or herb you have in abundance. In my garden, I usually pick more tansy than I need for other projects, so I use the extras for this tree. If you use a plant like artemisia with color along the whole stem, you will need far fewer stems. Or to cut down on total quantities, you can use a smaller wire form.

WHAT YOU NEED

200 stems of fresh-cut tansy, 6 inches long, with flowers and leaves

Additional dried flower heads or pods, including dried heliopsis flowers, acorns, paulownia pods, sensitive fern, and larch cones (optional)

Spiral wire topiary form, 27 inches tall

Jardiniere, clay pot, or other decorative pot, 8 to 12 inches tall, filled with soil

Small lazy Susan (optional)

Floral spool wire

Wire cutters

Hot glue gun and glue sticks

WHAT YOU DO

1. Push the bottom prongs of the wire form securely into the soil so the form stands straight in the pot. Place the pot on the lazy Susan, if you are using one.

2. Tie the wire to the bottom of the topiary form.

3. Start with 1 or 2 pieces of tansy. Lay it along the bottom of the wire facing toward you. Wrap once very tightly with the wire.

4. Continue placing the tansy and wrapping in the same direction, turning the spiral as you work until you reach the top of the topiary form.

5. As you near the top, use smaller pieces of tansy so the spiral seems to diminish into a point.

6. When finished with the spiral, cut the wire, leaving an end 6 inches long, and tie it off at the top.

7. Let the whole construction dry for about five days in a warm, dark, dry place.

8. Fill in any bare spots with additional tansy; hot-glue in place. If desired, decorate with additional dried flowers or pods, all glued directly to the tansy base. Graduate the size of the decorations, using larger pieces at the bottom and smaller ones as you go up the spiral.

Variation: Buy or pick quantities of Spanish moss to cover the wire form. Stretch out the moss into long strands about 2 inches thick and lay them against the spiral. Wrap with the wire, omitting the tansy altogether. Decorate with dried flowers as described in Step 8, choosing flowers that will be bright and will show up well against the gray background.

Step 3

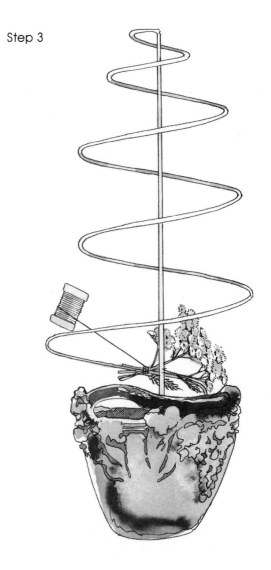

PROJECT POINTERS

Harvesting

Use freshly picked tansy for this project. It will not be brittle the way dried flowers would be, and the stems will bend easily and dry on the frame.

Tea Wreath

Create a Tea Wreath with materials that are both decorative and delicious. While I don't expect you'll want to rip it apart for the pot come tea time, the sight of it hanging on a kitchen wall will warm the heart of any tea drinker. Try giving a tea wreath as a housewarming or shower gift and get ready for thanks in profusion.

WHAT YOU NEED

About 40 bunches of dried herbs, with 6 to 8
    stems per bunch, including chamomile,
    bergamot, applemint, and rose hips
22- or 24-gauge floral spool wire
Floral wrapping tape (optional)
Wire cutters
Flat wire wreath frame, 16 inches in diameter
Pruning shears
3 tea infusers

WHAT YOU DO

1. Using an 8-inch piece of the wire and the tape, if desired, attach a wire hanger to mark the top of the wreath frame. See Appendix B on page 146 for instructions on making and attaching wire hangers.

2. Tie the end of the wire to the wreath frame.

3. Spread out the bunches of herbs on your work table and make your plan before you start the actual construction. That way you will avoid both creating a haphazard look and running out of material when you are almost finished. Since you will be wiring the bunches to the wreath form in groups of three, make your plan in trios. Take three small bunches of herbs; lay them on the wreath frame, one in the middle, the other two fanned out on the sides.

4. Wrap the stems tightly with the wire. Do not cut off the wire.

5. Take the next three bunches of herbs. Lay them over the first three, overlapping those stems. Wrap the new stems with the wire.

6. Continue around the wreath frame in this manner until it is completely covered with herbs.

7. The last three bunches will be the hardest because you have to hide the stems under the original three herb bunches. Wire these in place.

8. Cut off the wire from the spool, leaving a 6-inch end. Loop this end tightly to the back of the frame several times, to "tie off" the wire so it won't unravel.

9. Loop a piece of wire securely to the tea infusers. Space them evenly around the wreath.

Attach each to the wreath frame by slipping the wire through the flowers to the back of the frame and looping securely several times.

Step 4

PROJECT POINTERS

Drying

Many of the herbs are brittle when dried and will flake heavily if you try to separate the stems in a bunch. To help alleviate this problem, hang the herbs for this project in very small bunches (six to eight stems each) to dry, each wrapped in its rubber band. In constructing the wreath, use each bunch "as is," still in its rubber band wrap.

Wisteria Arch

Deeply gnarled, heavily entwined wisteria vine is an intriguing alternative to grape vine for wreath-making. Air-dried wisteria blooms and silica-dried dogwood "blossoms" (actually the colored, petal-like bracts) add an unusual touch to this project. While you can hang an arch wreath directly on a door, its shape makes it particularly appealing over a door, window, or mirror.

Step 4

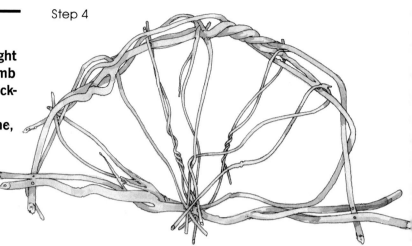

WHAT YOU NEED

32-inch-long vine of fresh-cut wisteria, as straight
   as possible and the thickness of your thumb
55-inch-long vine of fresh-cut wisteria, the thickness of your thumb
Assorted other pieces of fresh-cut wisteria vine,
   pencil thickness and slimmer
5 stems of dried blue or white hydrangea
About 11 bunches of dried wisteria flower
   panicles, with 5 to 6 stems per bunch
8 dried blossoms of pink or white dogwood
Hammer
1 dozen 1-inch brads
Hot glue gun and glue sticks, or thick white craft
   glue
Branch loppers
Pruning shears
6 inches of 22- or 24-gauge floral spool wire
Floral wrapping tape (optional)

WHAT YOU DO

1. Have your hammer and brads handy. Lay out the 32-inch vine in front of you. This will become the bottom of the arch. Next take the 55-inch vine and bend it to form the arch. Lay that out on the straight piece to check the curve. Let the straight and the curved pieces extend about 3 inches out from where they cross.

2. When you are generally pleased with the result, nail the vines together with the brads.

3. Now that the arch form is secure and sturdy, wind thinner pieces of vine around it. If you weave over and under the arch, the thinner pieces of vine will probably stay in place. If you need to, glue the ends of these pieces to hold them.

4. Cut five pieces of vine to various lengths, averaging about 15 inches long. Find the center of the "straight" bottom vine. Glue the bottoms of all of the smaller vine pieces to this center of the straight vine, fanning them out like spokes in a wheel. Glue the tops of the shortest vine "spokes" to the arch, and loop the tops of the longer spokes around the top of the arch, then wind them back around the bottom parts.

5. Trim off any unruly pieces with the branch loppers. Cheat a little—glue on any small sections of vine needed to even out the design.

6. Using 8 inches of the wire and the tape, if using, make a wire hanger and attach it to the center of the arch. See Appendix B on page 146 for instructions on making and attaching wire hangers.

7. Now you're ready to decorate. Glue on the stems of hydrangea to the bottom of the form, fanning out to follow the direction of the spokes.

8. Glue on the bunches of wisteria panicles, letting them droop down from the arch to mimic the way they grow. Glue on the dogwood blossoms as desired.

PROJECT POINTERS

Drying

Wisteria air dries well simply by hanging. Cut short stems in half bloom, bunch, and hang in a warm, dry place. With Chinese wisteria (*Wisteria sinensis*) the leaves unfurl after the panicle is almost in full bloom. Strip off any leaves before you dry the flowers, since the foliage adds little to the look of the dried bunches.

Cut newly opened pink or white dogwood blossoms and bury them in silica gel for about two weeks. Use them to decorate this and other craft projects. Be prepared for the inevitable comment, "They're so beautiful, they don't look real."

Dried Topiary Tree

Topiary, the art of training and shaping living plants into interesting forms, is a fascinating project for the dedicated gardener. In the home, creating topiaries with dried materials provides some of the same satisfactions without years of labor. At 2½ feet high, this colorful topiary tree is quite dramatic. Decorate your tree in colors to complement its surroundings.

WHAT YOU NEED

Green sphagnum moss or sheet moss, enough to cover the ball and the container top
10 stems of fresh-cut horsetail, 16 inches long
14 stems of fresh-cut horsetail, 6 to 8 inches long
16 dried pink strawflowers
5 large dried rose blossoms
8 tiny dried rosebuds
64 small dried pink globe amaranth heads
36 dried shrub rose blossoms
Terra-cotta container, old or new, about 9 inches high
1 brick of brown floral foam
10 pieces of 16-gauge floral spool wire, each 16 inches long
3 pieces of 24-gauge floral spool wire, each 6 to 8 inches long
Wire cutters
Jar or can
Styrofoam ball, 8 inches in diameter
15 greening pins
Spray adhesive
Hot glue gun and glue sticks

WHAT YOU DO

1. To prepare the terra-cotta container, wedge the brick of floral foam down into the container so it holds firm. It doesn't need to hit the bottom of the container as long as it is wedged in tightly.

2. Cover the top of the container with the moss, to hide the foam.

3. To create the stem, insert a piece of #16-gauge wire in the hollow stem of one 16-inch stem of horsetail. It will go in easily. Repeat with the other nine 16-inch stems.

4. Take three 6- to 8-inch pieces of fresh horsetail and insert a piece of #24-gauge wire into each of the hollow stems.

5. Make a bundle in your hand of the ten 16-inch-long wired stems, and tie them in three places with the three shorter wired stems.

6. Stand the tied bundle of stems in a jar or can and let dry for several days.

7. After drying, insert the bundle of stems upright in the center of the topiary container, pushing gently but firmly into the foam.

8. Next, prepare the head of the topiary. Use your wire cutters to poke a hole in the ball about 1½ inches deep and about 1 inch wide (wide enough to accommodate the tips of the stems when dried). This hole will mark the bottom of the ball, where you will insert the stems to form the trunk of the topiary.

9. Wrap the ball with sheet moss or sphagnum, covering all of the ball except for the hole. As you wrap, secure with greening pins pushed all the way through the moss into the Styrofoam. They will be invisible after the project is complete.

10. When the ball is completely wrapped, spray it with adhesive and roll it lightly around on your work table. The adhesive will make any little wisps of moss adhere to the ball, giving a smoother look to the finished topiary.

11. Attach the ball to the trunk. First try it on for size. Place the ball on the trunk to make sure the hole will fit when you glue the pieces together. Enlarge the hole if necessary.

12. Release a glob of hot glue into the hole in the ball. Let it set for 15 seconds to harden slightly, so the glue won't all run down when you invert the ball. Invert the ball over the trunk, and gently but firmly push the trunk into the hole in the ball. You want the trunk to pierce the ball. The glue is just an extra device to help make a secure connection.

13. Now you can decorate the ball. This decoration calls for a small topknot of flowers at the ball's "north pole" (see Step 14) and four scallops of flowers around the sides (see Step 15). The flowers are glued onto the moss.

14. To make the topknot, glue on four strawflowers in an X shape. Put one large rose blossom on top of the strawflowers. Fill in the spaces between the strawflowers with two tiny rosebuds and two globe amaranth heads.

15. To make the scallops, glue on the remaining four large rose blossoms at equal distances around the ball. Looking down on the topiary from above will help you find the right placement. The roses are about 4 inches down from the north pole.

16. For each scallop, add two rows of eight globe amaranth heads with a row of nine shrub rose blossoms between them. Fill in the spaces around the four large rose blossoms with the 12 remaining strawflowers and the six remaining rosebuds.

17. Add some accent stems to the pot. Take the remaining 11 short pieces of wired horsetail and insert them into the foam, pushing them in at an angle from the main trunk.

Step 17

Step 3

Step 14

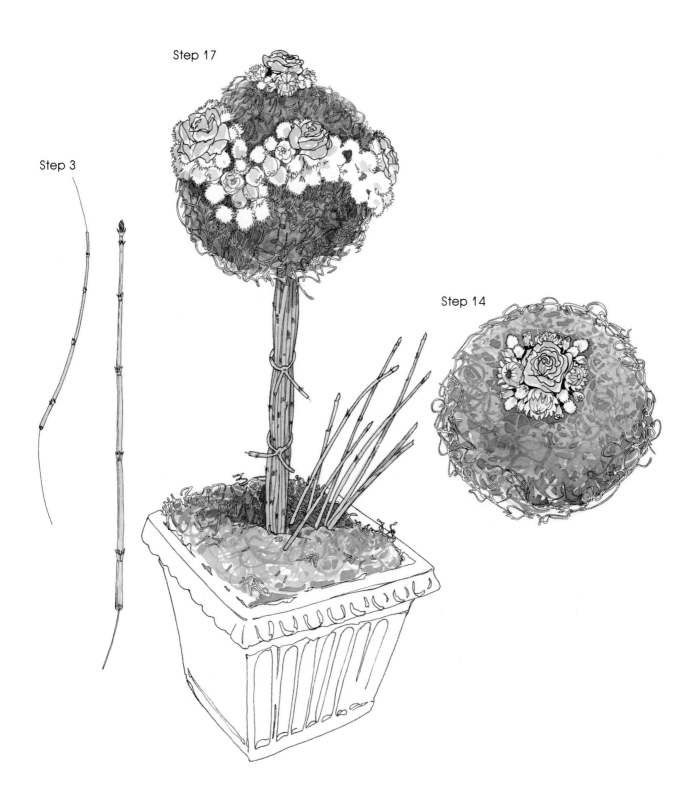

PROJECT POINTERS

Growing

Horsetail (*Equisetum hymale*) spreads rampantly through underground roots. Plant in a heavy metal container or tub or in a suitable location away from your main garden. Or you can buy it by the bunch from a florist.

Start strawflowers (*Helichrysum bracteatum*) indoors to get a jump on the season and to have a longer period for harvesting. Or if you're not in a hurry, sow them directly in the garden where you want them to grow. If you order through a catalog, you can often get seeds separated by color, or you can just buy a mix and get a range of colors. Unless you enjoy bending over to harvest your flowers, I suggest you forgo the short-stemmed 'Bikini' cultivars and select those that grow to at least 3 feet tall; I promise that you'll thank yourself at harvest time!

If you plan to harvest a lot of strawflowers, the cutting garden is the best place for them. Harvest each bloom for drying as soon as it has opened halfway. You can also cut some and place the stems in water for use as long-lasting fresh flowers. Adults and children alike are fascinated by the papery texture of the flowers.

Drying

Horsetail makes a wonderful accent in fresh or dried arrangements and when wired through the hollow stems, it can be bent in any direction. Always wire and bend while fresh. Let dry in the desired shape.

If you prefer not to use horsetail for this project, fresh bamboo would also be lovely. Or use any natural stick with an interesting bark, cut to the proper length.

Construction

For those who want a much easier project, there is now a topiary form that is available at most places where dried flowers are sold. It is a three-in-one basic form with a bottom (pot-shaped foam), a dowel stick for the trunk, and a foam ball for the head. You can trim the bottom foam to fit any pot you have. Cover the dowel stick with moss to make it look more natural; use your hot glue gun or thick white craft glue for this purpose. The top topiary ball is smaller than the one used in this project, but you can use the same pattern to decorate it and achieve a pleasing effect with much less work.

If you decide to use a terra-cotta container for your topiary tree, you'll need to decide what effect you want from it. Some people prefer their containers to look new, and they will soak and scrub old containers with vinegar to remove any encrusted white minerals that have accumulated over the years. Others will take brand-new containers and age them to achieve an "antique" finish. To age new terra-cotta quickly, soak the pot in water, remove it, and smear it with unflavored natural yogurt. Brush some soil on top of the yogurt, and put the pot outside under a bush or in some other dark, damp place. After about a month, molds and sometimes moss will grow on the surface of the pot. The colors you achieve will depend on the naturally occurring fungi in your area.

THE AUTUMN GARDEN

Fall really starts when school begins and not on September 22 as the calendar would have us believe. The parade of golden school buses two days after Labor Day signals the beginning of my fall garden planting and harvesting.

I plant miniature 'Tête-à-tête' daffodil bulbs and 'Apricot Beauty' tulips for winter forcing and stow them in my old basement fridge for a period of rest. The amaryllis are brought in from outside and sit in the dark for a period of dormancy. The Christmas cactus is now loaded with buds, so I retrieve it from its summer home under a shrub. Indoors, I display it on a pedestal to show off its mass of bloom. Some of my favorite fall projects involve bringing plants indoors to enjoy. I carefully select the tender herbs to dig and overwinter on my sun porch. Since space is very limited, only the favorites survive the final culling: bay, rosemary, and maybe a lemon verbena or two, if they promise not to have whitefly this year.

Outdoors, the orange pods of Chinese lanterns are always a sure sign of fall. These perennials are easy to grow from seed, or you can probably get divisions from a neighbor. Once established, these plants spread from creeping underground stems, so I plant them in a container or in an isolated garden bed to keep them under control. The lanterns are wonderful for all kinds of craft projects, and they are easy to work with either fresh (they'll dry in place) or already dried. They do not continue to ripen once picked. If you want them to be totally orange, be patient. I check the stems every few days until I see the bright orange color I'm looking for, and then I store the ripened stems in the barn.

I don't overdo the garden cleanup, partly out of laziness and partly to protect the seeds which will volunteer throughout my garden in the spring. I wait for the spring treat of finding plants which overwinter despite their catalog listing as annuals.

Putting a garden to bed also means seed saving. All summer I mean to do it but rarely find the time. Now there is no time for further delay. I hurry to collect and separate the cleome and celosia seeds by color, and shake out enough cosmos, bachelor's-buttons, sorghum, and okra to last me for next year. Not as adventurous as some when it comes to saving seeds, I hesitate to risk a complete crop failure, but each year I save several additional kinds to experiment with.

In addition to the usual fall planting and cleanup, I take this time to anticipate the materials I'll need for winter crafting. Like a squirrel, I search for cones, sweet-gum balls, nuts, and pods, selecting and storing ones that look promising for new projects. Gathering in the woods and fields means going out before hunting season starts, because I am fearful even in my neon red poncho and hat as the shots ring out around me. I collect wild rose hips, sumac, mosses, fern pods, some dried fungus and bark on downed trees, still-pliable grape and other vines, and bittersweet.

In the garden, I pick the last of the roses, zinnias, delphiniums, and other special flowers, and bury them in silica gel to be removed when the house is no longer humid. Most of the crops must be picked before the first frost, even if there will be many warm days to follow. One year my 300-foot row of celosia blackened overnight as an unexpected early frost rimed Orwigsburg, Pennsylvania, on September 22. I press goldenrods, hydrangeas, colored leaves, a few mums, and other fall foliage and flowers to round out my already abundant collection.

Bittersweet Wreath and Harvest Sheaf

Enjoy the beauty and bounty of fall with these quick and easy crafts. The Harvest Sheaf (*bottom*) makes a dramatic arrangement in any setting. Sorghum is my favorite for this project, but you can use almost any grain. The Bittersweet Wreath (*top*) is a creative way to use a plant that is often considered a weed. Within days of picking, the hulls on this vine pop open, exposing the bright orange berries within.

Bittersweet Wreath

WHAT YOU NEED

8 or more stems of fresh-cut, nicely fruited, early bittersweet, at least 4 feet long

WHAT YOU DO

1. Strip most of the leaves from each stem of bittersweet.

2. This wreath is woven just using the stems. Start with your longest stem. Hold it at the thicker end with your left hand. With your right hand, form a circle with about ¾ of the stem, and clasp it at the top with your left hand.

3. Wrap the remainder of the stem in and out along the circle you have formed. When you are finished, the circle should hold by itself. This is the wreath base.

4. Take the longest remaining stem and wrap in and out along the weakest part of the wreath base until you have used up that branch. The berries usually grow along only part of the stem, so as you continue with your wrapping, try to even out the placement of the berries along the wreath.

5. Continue this process with each stem, wrapping around the outside and weaving in and out of any gaps. Once you have woven a branch, you can make corrections by adding rather than removing.

6. The finished project will have a wonderful wild and natural look. Hang the wreath the same day and let the wreath finish drying in place. Don't hang the finished project on a heavily used door, because the dry berries will drop if brushed against or if the door is slammed.

PROJECT POINTERS

Growing

In some areas of the Northeast, bittersweet is now considered a noxious weed, growing rampant along roadsides and strangling deciduous trees. To me, bittersweet, more than any other plant, signals the glories of fall. If you plant your own bittersweet vines, you'll need both male and female plants to get fruit.

Harvesting

Bittersweet that is picked too green will never ripen. Look for the faintest tinge of gold on the hull—a signal that it will ripen rapidly after picking. If you're picking in the wild, beware of poison ivy, which often grows near bittersweet.

I try to rush the season by picking bittersweet around Labor Day when the berries are just starting to turn from green to gold, the hulls are still closed, and the stems are pliable. Whether you buy or pick your own bittersweet, the secret to working with this vine is freshness. When the stems are very fresh (within three days of picking), they can easily be shaped. After they get brittle, don't even bother trying.

Warning: Bittersweet berries are poisonous if eaten. If you have toddlers or babies in the crawling stage, wait a few years before bringing bittersweet into the house.

Step 4

Harvest Sheaf

WHAT YOU NEED

75 thin stems of dried sorghum, about 2½ feet
  tall
2 strands of raffia
2 yards of twisted paper ribbon
Heavy-duty scissors or pruning shears
6 inches of 26-gauge floral spool wire

WHAT YOU DO

1. Take about half of the stems of sorghum,
align the heads, and holding the clump in one
hand, trim the bottoms as evenly as possible with
the scissors or pruning shears.

2. Lay the bundle on a work table or floor.
With one strand of raffia, tie the bundle as tightly
as possible a few inches below the heads, wrapping the raffia around the bundle several times to
hold it securely.

3. Stand the bundle up and give it several
thumps on the table to even up the base. At this
point it should be able to stand on its own.

4. Holding the bundle in your left hand, add
the rest of the sorghum stems around the bundle,
distributing as evenly as possible and aligning
the heads.

5. Wrap and tie the remaining strand of raffia around this thicker bundle a few inches below
the heads to hold it securely. Then put one hand
around the neck of the bundle near the tie and
one hand around the bundle near the bottom,
and twist in opposite directions, as though you
were wringing out wash. This wringing process
gives the spiral line to the bundle.

6. Now comes the hardest part—the final
trim of the stem bottoms. The center stems should
still be even from the first trim. The outer stems
will splay out in a spiral and should be left slightly
longer to support the base. Trim carefully with
the scissors or pruning shears, and check frequently to have a firm-standing bundle.

7. In the final shaping, you can gently pull
up some of the middle heads to make a peak.
Even if you have tied your raffia very tightly,
there will be a little "play" to allow for this.

8. Make a bow with the ribbon and the wire,
and attach it to the sheaf with the wire. See

Appendix A on page 144 for complete bow-
making instructions.

Variation: If you don't want to grow or buy the
sorghum, a readily accessible grass like foxtail
creates a graceful bundle with a slightly different
look. The foxtail is shorter and thinner than the
sorghum, so many more stalks will be needed. One
can find it in the Northeast growing everywhere
from cornfields to roadsides to sidewalk cracks in
city pavement. The construction steps are the
same as above, only tie the bundle higher on the
stalk, just under the seed head, for best effect.

Step 5

PROJECT POINTERS

Growing

Though you can substitute almost any grain for this project, I find that the large seed heads and thick stalks of sorghum make it the easiest material to work with. If you are unfamiliar with sorghum, you are not alone. Few visitors to my farm recognize it growing in the field or hanging to dry in my barn. It is, however, an extremely versatile crop. Sorghum seeds can be cooked or ground into flour, and the stems are used to make a sweet syrup. On farms where sorghum is grown, children often chew on pieces of the stalk like sugarcane. And, of course, its decorative uses are endless.

Before I started to grow my own sorghum, I was attracted to the beauty of the growing stalks in some neighboring fields. I was able to beg some from the farmer to try a few projects, and when the results were pleasing, I sought the seed for my garden. The local feed store sold only 50-pound bags, about 48 pounds more than I needed. Though they promised me any spillage from broken bags, I was afraid to count on an accident. Fortunately, I found that the Bountiful Gardens catalog is an excellent source for small quantities of grain seeds. (For their address, see page 154.)

Harvesting

Sorghum seed heads look attractive at many different stages, starting with beige flowers and then green seeds that ripen to white. Don't wait until the seeds are fully ripe to pick the stalks because the seeds will drop off.

Drying

Sorghum can be bunched and hung or spread on screens to dry. Do not remove the leaves—they stay a pale celery green and add a lovely hue to any arrangement.

If you have mice, as I do in my barn, be careful to store your sorghum and other grains in mouse-proof containers, or in the springtime you will find a lovely pile of stalks and dust with no seed heads attached.

Autumn Candle Holders

Colorful squash and gourds are naturals for fall decorating. Add a few candles and some ivy vines to create a stunning arrangement for a living room coffee table or the Thanksgiving dinner table. It is impossible to tell how long each squash will last (it could be anywhere from two weeks to six months), so use this project like a fresh arrangement for a special occasion.

WHAT YOU NEED

3 strands of fresh-cut English ivy, each about 2 feet long

3 fresh 'Turk's Turban' or other ornamental squash of different sizes with colorful markings

2 smaller fresh ornamental squash of complementary colors

Sharp knife

1 used candle

Matches

Corkscrew

Heavy-duty scissors or pruning shears

3 candle prongs

3 ivory or white candle tapers, 15 inches tall

Protective spray (optional)

WHAT YOU DO

1. Condition the ivy by completely submerging it in a basin of warm water for 24 hours.

2. Make sure that each squash sits level on the table. If one doesn't, use the knife to slice a small bit off of the bottom, and seal the fresh cut by dripping hot candle wax from the used candle all over the cut. Set aside the two smaller squash.

3. With the knife, remove the stems of the three larger squash. With the corkscrew, drill a small starter hole in the stem end of each of the three squash.

4. Use the scissors or shears to trim off the corners of the square bases of the candle prongs. This will make the plastic less noticeable in your finished arrangement.

5. Press a candle prong firmly into the starter hole of each squash. Set a taper in each candle holder.

6. Wrap a strand of ivy around the candle base. Weave the ivy in and out to hold one end, and let the other trail across the table. After the ivy is arranged, apply protective spray to it, if desired, to further extend the life of the ivy. Be careful not to let your tapers burn down and touch the material at the base!

7. Complete the arrangement by grouping the squash in a pleasing configuration and adding the two smaller squash.

Variations: Use other gourds, pumpkins, and squash with contrasting candles. For example, try three pattypan squash sitting on a base of purple and red pressed fall leaves with deep wine-colored candles. Or try an apple arrangement. Take five large red apples and make a hole through the core of each apple at the blossom end with a potato peeler. Insert a thin, apple-green or rose-colored candle taper firmly in each hole. Set the apples on the table. If any are unsteady, slice a tiny bit off the bottom and seal the entire cut area with hot wax dripped from a used candle. Also seal the cut area where the candle is inserted into the apple. This will help preserve the fruit and stave off fruit flies. Arrange the apples on pressed grape leaves and twine bare grapevine around the grouping.

PROJECT POINTERS

Growing

'Turk's Turban' squash are easy to grow from seed. One pack can give you enough to decorate for a large party or to give to friends. If you live in an area with a short growing season, start your seeds indoors in peat pots about a month before the last frost date. Otherwise, plant them directly in the garden about a week after the last frost date, when the weather has settled and the soil is getting warm. They prefer a light and well-drained but moisture-retentive soil. Keep the seedlings well watered and weeded. Once the vines start to lengthen, you can apply a thick mulch of straw to keep the weeds down. If cucumber beetles attack your plants, handpick the pests from the leaves or spray the leaves with pyrethrin or sabadilla.

Harvesting

Pick squash when its stem begins to dry. Harvest the squash carefully to avoid bruising or nicking the flesh. Use a knife to cut the squash from the main vine, along with a few inches of the stem.

❧ Baby Pumpkin Patch

Relive the fun of childhood scavenger hunts by creating a Baby Pumpkin Patch for your home. For the arrangement shown in the photo above, I've included some of my favorite fall finds, such as glossy horse chestnuts, brown spore stalks of sensitive fern, rosy red kousa dogwood fruit, green mimosa tree seedpods, and a variety of acorns, accented by red crab apples and bright orange baby pumpkins.

WHAT YOU NEED

Fresh or dried Spanish moss
20 fresh miniature pumpkins, like 'Jack Be Little'
Assortment of fresh or dried seeds, nuts, seedpods, and fruits of autumn
Sharp knife
4 bricks of brown floral foam
Low, wide basket
5 to 7 small terra-cotta flowerpots, in assorted sizes from 2 to 4 inches wide, with drainage holes
Floral clay
7 floral prongs
10 to 14 small sticks, to fit through the flowerpot holes

WHAT YOU DO

1. Using the knife, cut the floral foam into blocks of different heights, making one block for beneath each flowerpot. Check to see that the rims of the pots are visible above the rim of the basket when they're sitting on the foam blocks.

2. Secure the foam to the basket by placing a small piece of floral clay at the bottom of each floral prong, sticking the prongs to the bottom of the basket, and impaling each piece of cut foam on a prong.

Step 4

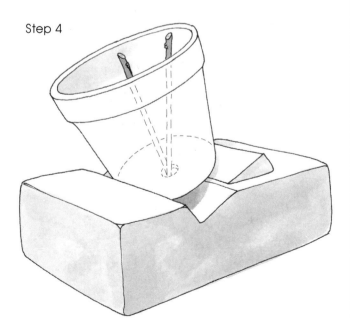

3. Stand one pot on a foam block, tilting the pot slightly outward. Put a sliver of foam (about ½ inch wide) under the back of the pot to maintain the tilt. Cut an indentation in the foam block (about ¼ inch deep) under the front of the pot to help keep the pot in place.

4. Secure the pot by pushing two sticks through the holes in the bottom of the pot and into the foam. Repeat Steps 3 and 4 with the remaining flowerpots.

5. Stretch out the Spanish moss to make it less dense and use it to hide all the floral foam.

6. Scatter the miniature pumpkins around in a pleasing way, filling in the empty spaces between the pots. Intersperse with crab apples or other fruits.

7. Move the basket from your work table to its final resting place. Once you fill the pots, it is tricky to move the basket without toppling the piles.

8. Fill each pot with a different fruit or nut.

9. Without disturbing the overall design, you can replace the contents of the pots as the season progresses and the materials fade or shrivel. This way, the arrangement can last from early fall until well past Thanksgiving.

PROJECT POINTERS

Growing

Miniature pumpkins are a fine crop for children to plant. The seeds are large and easy to handle, and the vines grow quickly; the progress from blossom to tiny green fruit to ripened vegetable is easy to follow. Best of all, the harvested fruit lasts many months indoors. Display them in a container, or allow children to use them as objects for creative play.

Harvesting

You can combine any fruits and nuts in this design and have a good excuse for an autumn jaunt in the country or a scavenger hunt along city streets or in a local farmers' market. Besides the materials mentioned in this project, you could include yellow hardy orange fruit, kumquats, red magnolia fruit, lady apples, cotoneaster berries, orange or yellow pyracantha berries—the list is endless.

Seasonal Vases

Combining flowers and vegetables makes a lavish but inexpensive display for any part of your home. The vegetable vases will last at least as long as the flowers (about a week); they are not meant to be permanent. A cool atmosphere will help both the vases and the flowers last longer.

WHAT YOU NEED

Fresh-cut fall flowers, including 'Autumn Joy' sedum, asters, ageratum, goldenrods, calendulas, delphiniums, bachelor's-buttons, blue sages, yarrows, and pokeberries
Colorful array of fresh fall vegetables and gourds, including hubbard and crookneck squash, red and yellow bell peppers, and cauliflower
Bucket full of tepid water
Sharp knife
Small glass baby food and jelly jars
Green floral foam

WHAT YOU DO

1. Remove leaves from the bottom of the flower stems and condition by standing flowers in a bucket of deep, tepid water for at least 3 hours. Note: Don't use pokeberry in your arrangements if you have small children—its seeds and roots are poisonous.

2. To make a pepper vase, use the knife to cut out the stem of a firm bell pepper. Make a hole about 1½ inches wide and remove the seeds and pith. If you take care not to pierce the bottom skin, the pepper can hold water, but I prefer to insert a tiny jar as a liner and add water. Alternatively, cut saturated floral foam to size and insert in the opening. Fill the jar or foam with one kind of flower, like fall asters or mums, with the stems cut short (about 6 to 9 inches long).

3. For the squash vase, find the best side of a hubbard or crookneck squash by checking for balance, flaws, and color. The squash vase can either lie down or stand upright. Cut a hole about 4 inches in diameter in the top or side; cut through to the hollow center. With your hand, remove and discard all seeds and fibers that you can. Rinse out the vegetable cavity. Insert a jar in the hole so it stands securely and add water, or cut a block of saturated floral foam and insert in the hole. Arrange a natural-looking bouquet of flowers in the jar or foam. Add water daily.

4. To make a vase out of a cauliflower, carefully carve a hole about 3 inches in diameter and 3 inches deep in the side of the vegetable. Insert a piece of saturated floral foam. Add flowers that are not heavy drinkers, like goldenrod.

Variation: Use a pumpkin as a vase. Cut off the top to make a lid and clean out the insides. Insert a large brick of saturated floral foam (two or more blocks if the pumpkin is very large). With a paring knife, carefully cut out three or more 3-inch holes in random places around the sides of the pumpkin. Each hole can contain a bunch of flowers, with the stems reaching through to the foam. Either close the lid or insert flowers in the top.

PROJECT POINTERS

Growing

The shorter days of fall are a great time in the garden. As the night temperature hovers near freezing, the garden puts on a last show of brilliant color. The snapdragons and calendulas that languished in the summer heat now grow tall and vibrant. Autumn bloomers like orange-flowered lion's-ear (*Leonotis leonurus*) and pink-flowering showy stonecrop (*Sedum spectabile*) are at their peaks. And if you deadhead them regularly, many spring and early-summer perennials will reward you with a second (though less prolific) flush of flowers in fall.

Even after the first several frosts, your flower garden can still yield an abundant harvest. If you look around, you're sure to find some materials that can contribute to a colorful indoor arrangement. Even as late as Thanksgiving Day, after a number of severe frosts, I can usually find some less-than-perfect chrysanthemums and snapdragons to make a small table arrangement.

Since I concentrate on growing flowers, I look to the farmers' market for piles of magnificent vegetables and squash to use as vases. There I puzzle the vendors by inspecting for balance, shape, and color. It's worth the few extra minutes (and the strange looks) to get a vase that is attractive and well balanced.

Design

The vibrant colors of the seasonal vases augment whatever flowers are available. The blend of flowers and vegetables makes a lavish but inexpensive display that you can use for a large party or reception.

Teapot Arrangement

There are few places in the house that won't look more welcoming with an arrangement of dried flowers in a teapot. Grouping each kind of flower, as shown in the photo above, highlights the beauty of the flowers and doesn't tax the skill of the arranger. For a fall arrangement in a copper pot, yellows, blues, lavenders, grays, and whites are pleasing.

WHAT YOU NEED

A handful of Spanish moss

3 to 8 stems each of blue hydrangea, delphinium, globe thistle, fern, immortelle, strawflowers, allium flowerheads, roses, and *Helipterum humboldtianum*

Floral prong

Wide-mouth teapot or teakettle

Floral clay

Sharp knife

Brick of brown floral foam

Scissors or pruning shears

Step 5

WHAT YOU DO

1. Attach the floral prong to the bottom of the teapot with a small bit of floral clay.

2. With the knife, cut the floral foam to fit the opening of the teapot. The height should extend above the rim by 1 inch.

3. Trim off the corners of the top of the foam with the knife, to give a slightly rounded appearance.

4. Spread the Spanish moss loosely over the foam and have it droop down the sides of the teapot.

5. Beginning with one variety of flower, use scissors or pruning shears to trim the stems to an even length and insert them into the side of the foam in one area, coming up over the top. The length of the stems will depend on the size teapot you're using. For a 4- to 6-cup teapot, keep the stems 3 to 5 inches long. The longer the stems, the more flowers you'll need for a compact arrangement.

6. Continue with each kind of flower, inserting the stems in a cluster.

Variation: Use an English-style trug or harvest basket to make a patchwork arrangement. No foam is needed, just many bunches of flowers, all with the stems cut short (4 to 6 inches long). Vary the shapes, colors, and textures of the flowers; add groups of moss or twigs as desired. Release each bunch gently from its rubber band or string wrapping and stand it up next to its neighbor. Massing the flowers in the arrangement helps them to support each other and keeps the flowers in place.

PROJECT POINTERS

Growing

The perennial globe thistle (*Echinops ritro*) is useful in fresh or dried bouquets. It will often bloom the first year from seed started indoors. Plants can grow 4 to 5 feet high and 4 feet wide, so give them plenty of room. In my experience, the cultivar 'Taplow Blue' is too fragile after drying to be useful, although the species is normally quite sturdy when dried.

Cotton Wreath

W hen I saw this cotton welting rolled up in an upholstery shop, it demanded to be felt and cuddled. I found the combination of airy softness and speckled texture irresistible. This simple wrapped wreath features cotton bolls as decoration, along with dried okra, teasel, and martynia pods. The light colors of the materials show up beautifully against any dark background.

WHAT YOU NEED

5 yards of 1½-inch-diameter, uncovered cotton
    welting
2 martynia pods
2 okra pods
4 teasel pods
3 cotton bolls (optional)
Flat wire wreath frame, 18 inches in diameter
Hot glue gun and glue sticks, or thick white craft
    glue
Scissors

WHAT YOU DO

1. Wrap the cotton welting around the wreath frame. To start, lay 3 inches of the end of the welting horizontally along the center of the frame. Hold this with one hand. Begin to wrap around the frame, covering this end first.

2. Continue to wrap around the frame, keeping an even tension on the welting and completely covering the frame. You should have about 1 yard left to make a decorative knot.

Step 1

3. Cut off the excess welting, leaving 3 inches in the back of the wreath. Tuck this small piece under the last three wraps to finish off and secure the welting.

4. Make a simple knot with the excess welting. Since it is composed of many separate strands held together with thin thread, release this thread to allow the strands to dangle freely.

5. Glue the knot on the side of the wreath.

6. Arrange the pods in a pleasing design, starting with the martynia, and glue in place. Next glue on the okra. The teasel is held by its own thorns, catching on the welting like Velcro. If you're using cotton bolls, glue them on last.

Variation: You can substitute any available pods for those suggested. Use catalpa or locust pods for curves, lotus for mass, and conifer cones or sweet-gum balls for accent.

PROJECT POINTERS

Growing

If you are adventurous, you might want to try growing your own cotton bolls, as I did. Since cotton is a 200-day crop, I started the seeds in flats on my windowsills in late February. Two packs of seeds dwindled down to eight plants set out in sandy soil in early May, protected by milk carton cloches (see the illustration on page 15 for more information on cloches). All summer long I enjoyed watching the delicate flowers bloom and the small green bolls form and swell.

Harvesting

When I grew my own cotton, I was forced to harvest it before the bolls were full size. By the beginning of October, only one boll had burst open, and we were on the verge of a killing frost. I picked all the remaining bolls and performed "surgery." With a small paring knife I slit them open along the four natural ridges and baked them on a cake rack in a 150°F oven for 3 hours. With a little prodding from a fork, the cotton burst out from the boll. If you look very carefully at the photo on the opposite page, you will see three very small cotton bolls near the knot. Next year I will graciously accept the kind offer of my friends from South Carolina to bring me cotton bolls for my crafts.

Hydrangea Basket and Lantern Wreath

The Hydrangea Basket (*bottom*) is the simplest kind of arrangement to make—an interesting container and an abundance of one kind of dried flower. Hydrangea is perfect for a large arrangement: one stem has both mass and delicacy, as well as a range of shades. The colorful Lantern Wreath (*top*) also has a simple design. It is accented with a sheaf of sorghum and a raffia bow.

Hydrangea Basket

WHAT YOU NEED

About 10 stems of heavily flowered fresh-cut or dried hydrangea with good color
An interesting basket

WHAT YOU DO

1. Place the stems of hydrangea in the container one by one, massing the flowers at different heights. Let a few heads droop down over the side.

2. Place the arrangement on a sunny windowsill or in a spot where it will greet you when you come through the front door.

PROJECT POINTERS

Growing

If you have the room, I recommend growing both the peegee hydrangea (*Hydrangea paniculata* 'Grandiflora') and 'Nikko Blue' hydrangea (*H. macrophylla* 'Nikko Blue') in your landscape. You'll get the dual benefits of enjoying the flowering shrubs for most of the summer and having the flowers to dry when they start to change color.

Harvesting

The only tricky part to drying hydrangea is knowing when to pick them. Even then, not every flower on the bush will mature at the same time, and you must be selective. Hydrangea flowers will not dry well unless they are mature. They actually start the drying process on the shrub, so pick when the color starts to change. The once pure-white florets will become cream, green, pink, and rose and the once vivid blues will fade slightly and turn to lavender, green, and wine. If you wait too long before picking, they will be a soft, uniform beige color, which is acceptable but much less interesting for craft work. Other signs of maturity are that the florets feel more papery and the flower heads give a rustling sound when shaken. In the Northeast, a few crisp nights in early September signal that the flowers of the peegee hydrangea will be ready. Blue hydrangeas usually mature several weeks earlier.

Lantern Wreath

WHAT YOU NEED

6 stems of sorghum, 22 inches long
About 70 individual fresh-cut or dried lanterns (a stem bears 2 to 5 lanterns)
2 strands of raffia
Scissors or pruning shears
Straw wreath base, 14 inches in diameter
2 greening pins
Hot glue gun and glue sticks, or thick white craft glue

WHAT YOU DO

1. Make a small bundle of the grain and tie it tightly with a raffia bow. With the scissors or pruning shears trim the ends of the stems neatly.

2. Place this bundle on one side of the wreath base. Pin it down securely with the greening pins. The ends of the bundle will extend past the top and bottom of the wreath.

3. Trim all the lantern stems flush with the bottoms of the lanterns.

4. Sort the lanterns into three piles by size: small, medium, and large. Start gluing the large lanterns on the face of the wreath base at the bottom of the raffia bow and moving clockwise around the wreath base. Glue the stem ends to the wreath, letting the lantern points stick up.

5. When the large lanterns are used up, continue the same process with the medium and small lanterns until you get around to the top of the bow. Don't worry about covering every spot of the wreath face, because the straw base looks attractive where it peeks out between the lanterns. Also, the wreath will look more interesting if you don't glue the lanterns in a completely regular pattern. Glue some lanterns bottom-side up, or cut open a few to expose the plump fruit inside. It's a good way to use up your damaged or less-ripe lanterns—the stem ends are usually more vivid than the tips.

Variation: Use the same method of construction as above, substituting about 40 dried gloriosa daisy flower heads for the lanterns. This wreath is also attractive with dried purple coneflowers.

Braided Bellpull and Versatile Flower Bows

Paper ribbon allows those of us who could never tie a decent bow to look like bow-making wizards. These projects are two ways you can use paper ribbon to create lovely accents for your home. Try the Versatile Flower Bow (*left*) or Braided Bellpull (*right*) to add color to a small space, to dress up a gift package, or to decorate a table or door.

Braided Bellpull

WHAT YOU NEED

Assorted plant materials, including German statice, foxtail, strawflowers, winged ever-lasting, globe amaranth, acorn caps, and hydrangea
8 yards of twisted paper ribbon
2 strands of raffia
Hot glue gun and glue sticks, or thick white craft glue
Scissors
Decorative hook or nail

WHAT YOU DO

1. Cut the paper ribbon into six lengths, each 4 feet long.

2. Untwist the paper ribbon. You can do this with the ribbon wet or dry. To relax the twist, soak in water for 15 minutes. Squeeze to elimi-nate most of the water, and gently untwist the ribbon. Hang over a shower rod to dry before you try to work with it. If you have a little patience, the ribbon is easy enough to untwist in its dry state, and you can work the ribbon to its full width.

3. Grasp the lengths of untwisted ribbon together about 6 inches from the top, make a loop, and pull the ends through to make a large knot.

4. Separate the ribbons into three sets, each consisting of two strands, and braid the three sets of strands from the knot end.

5. Stop braiding about 4 inches from the bottom. Wrap the unknotted end tightly with two strands of raffia and make a bow.

6. Glue on the flowers in five groupings. Start with the German statice. Cut the stems 3 to 4 inches long and glue them to the braid in each grouping. The ends of the flowers can be tucked into the braid to make a neat job.

7. Contine gluing the flowers into each grouping, starting with the larger flowers and ending with the smallest. There is no need to make each grouping identical, but the groupings will contain the same colors and kinds of flowers and so will be in harmony with one another. Keep a pattern in mind as you work. As you glue the

flowers to the braid, angle some of them out over the edges of the braid on either side. This process will make the finished design look more natural and free-flowing.

8. Trim the uneven end of the braid with your scissors.

9. Hang from a decorative hook or a nail.

Variation: If you use three strands of ribbon, each 2 yards long, the finished length will be about 4 feet, long enough and flexible enough to swag over a picture, mirror, wall clock, or small window. Decorate as above, increasing the number of flower groupings to nine. You can also use it as a festive runner down the center of a dining room table or make two and drape them from above a door frame down each side of the frame.

PROJECT POINTERS

Growing

German statice (*Goniolimon tataricum*) is also known as *Limonium tataricum* or *Statice tatarica;* you may find it in catalogs or garden centers under any of these names. This perennial is easy to grow. Buy healthy-looking container plants and plant them in full sun. These plants don't need a lot of fertilizer or other attention, and I haven't found them to have any disease or pest problems.

Drying

In my garden, German statice blooms in early July. I pick it when the tiny white, pink, or purple flower is visible, and the white bract is completely open. You don't need to hang this plant up to dry it—just stand it in a container in an out-of-the-way spot, or use it freshly cut in your arrangement and let it dry in place. When completely dried, the tiny flowers seem to disappear, but the showy white bracts remain. Use the stems whole, or break off small pieces for projects.

Construction

German statice is frequently used as filler material in dried bouquets. It is readily available for purchase, but buyer beware! While it is true that the flower can last for years, some shops sell blooms that are quite old. Freshly dried German statice looks sprightly, with white flowers (actually papery bracts) and bright green stems. By comparison, old German statice has off-white bracts and brown stems. Freshly dried flowers will make a valuable contribution to your craft projects, since their bright whites and greens are the two most important colors in making your arrangements fresh looking. Old flowers will make your arrangements look dull and tired.

Versatile Flower Bows

WHAT YOU NEED (for one bow)

Assorted plant materials, including German statice, foxtail, strawflowers, winged everlasting, globe amaranth, acorn caps, and hydrangea
2 yards of twisted paper ribbon
6 inches of 26-gauge floral spool wire
Hot glue gun and glue sticks, or thick white craft glue
Scissors

WHAT YOU DO

1. Untwist the paper ribbon. See Step 2 of the Braided Bellpull project on page 113 for complete instructions.

2. To make the bow, leave a tail about 1 foot long. Pinch the ribbon in your right hand and make a loop about 6 inches long. Continue to pinch the center of the loop with your right hand. With your left hand, make another 6-inch loop and pinch in the center with your right hand. Make two more loops, one to the right and one to the left, each about 5 inches long. Leave another long tail.

3. While you continue to pinch the bow in the center with one hand, wrap the wire tightly around the center of the bow.

Step 4

4. Release your hands now that the wire is securing the bow and perk out the loops into a pleasing shape. The glory of paper ribbon is that it stays where you put it but you can easily reshape it without making a crease. Use the ends of the wire, twisted to the back of the bow, for hanging.

5. Glue the flowers to the center of the bow, starting with the largest first. Glue the hydrangea stem directly to the paper ribbon, hiding the wire. The other flowers can be glued either to the ribbon or to the hydrangea. Allow some of the flowers to protrude from the top of the bow to give it more height.

6. Trim the ends of the ribbon on a slant to finish off the project.

PROJECT POINTERS

Drying

Hydrangea flowers are easy to dry and take just a few days. You can hang them, or just stand them in a cardboard box until the flower heads are crisp to the touch. There is no need to stand them in water, as is commonly recommended. Actually, though, I prefer to work with freshly picked hydrangea; it will dry in place without dropping petals.

THE WINTER GARDEN

The onset of cold weather brings a period of relief from daily gardening chores: no weeding, little planting, and few bugs to worry about. The flowering kale looks jewel-like with the morning frost, inspiring me to create a centerpiece that will incorporate several choice specimens in a design. It's the time for pruning and planning. Even when the weather turns frigid and the roads are covered with dirty snow, my mood is intensely optimistic. I fantasize about next year's garden: in my mind's eye, perfect in color, lush in growth and diversity.

The list of new seeds and plants I *must* have swells as I scour the pile of plant catalogs. I refer to my notes of ideas I have seen, read, or heard about during the year—of flowers that will dry well or of interesting plant combinations. I am seduced yet again by the catalog writer who finds another superlative to describe a new introduction. The photographer at White Flower Farms is to blame for that close-up of *Lilium auratum* 'Platyphyllum' that forces me to place an order even though we have quite enough lilies. I overorder every year, despite sturdy resolutions to the contrary and with full knowledge that at planting time I'll be muttering about my January weakness.

I've planned my winter garden carefully, so there will be materials of interest both in the landscape and for cutting. In addition to needle-leaved conifers and broad-leaved evergreens, like holly and rhododendron, I have planted red-twig dogwood for the brilliant crimson color of the stems against the snow. Contorted hazel has earned a place for the corkscrew shape of its leafless branches. I also have spring-flowering shrubs like forsythia, flowering quince, and pussy willow to cut on a brutally cold, dark January day and force into blossom on my living room windowsill.

At the Meadow Lark, craft work becomes frantic as my customers seek unusual Christmas presents. I also take special pleasure in planning my own holiday gifts for family and friends. This year, for example, a special few on my list will receive hand-colored antique botanical prints that I have matted and framed with a design of pressed flowers, leaves, and seeds. (If you'd like to create a pressed-flower project for yourself, see the Pressed-Flower Note Cards and Frames project on page 134.)

After the excitement of the holidays, take some time to relax and enjoy the outdoors. Late winter is a great time to go on a walk to hunt natural treasure, either in the country on in your own neighborhood. Perhaps you can cajole some children to go exploring with you. Equip each little hunter with a collecting bag, and arm the adults with pruning shears. Search for interesting natural objects to use in projects or in winter arrangements. Children will love to make a simple still life composition out of their best discoveries. It is not unusual to find an old bird's nest downed by a winter storm, some bark clinging to a dead tree limb, or a variety of cones and pods. If you don't need your treasures right away, clean and store them for later use when you need the perfect object to complete an arrangement.

When I go on a winter hunt with an eye out for new materials, I am always amazed how I suddenly notice things that I previously had just passed by. One cold February, I found some vivid green catbrier (*Smilax* sp.) growing among the brown underbrush along my usual walk. In the spring and summer, it is quite unnoticeable until the prickly stems reach out and grab you by the ankle. I was totally unaware that it stays a beautiful bright green in winter, and I picked some (with leather gloves) and wrapped it around itself to make an easy winter wreath for our front door.

117

Dried Fruit Wreath

Edibles and purely decorative plant material combine in this bountiful Dried Fruit Wreath reminiscent of colonial America. A range of dried fruits, including pomegranates and slices of apples, oranges, lemons, and grapefruit, accent the base of greens. Other materials include horse chestnuts, slices of Osage oranges, and pods of magnolias, okra, and poppies. Experiment with whatever materials you can find.

WHAT YOU NEED

48 bundles of fresh-cut greens, such as cedar, arborvitae, pine, or boxwood, with 4- to 6-inch stems, 3 to 5 stems per bundle

Assortment of dried fruits, vegetables, cones, and nuts, including pomegranates; slices of oranges, lemons, grapefruit, Osage oranges, and apples; mushrooms; horse chestnuts; and paulownia, okra, poppy, and magnolia pods

Flat wire wreath frame, 18 inches in diameter

Floral spool wire

Hot glue gun and glue sticks

4-inch floral picks

Brown floral wrapping tape

1 yard of wide decorative ribbon

WHAT YOU DO

1. To create the base, place three of the bundles of greens on the wreath frame, and wrap with the wire. Add three more bundles, so the tops overlap the bases of the three original bundles. Continue around the frame in this manner. Tuck the stems of the last bundles under the tops of the first ones.

2. Glue on one type of fruit or vegetable at a time, starting with the pomegranates. Then add the other large pieces like Osage orange slices and okra pods. Attach the magnolia pods with floral picks wrapped with the tape.

3. Glue on apple and citrus slices, then the nuts and other materials. Tie the ribbon to the top of the back of your wreath. Tie the ribbon ends into a pretty bow several inches from where the ribbon attaches to the wreath. Hang your wreath from the ribbon.

PROJECT POINTERS

Growing

'Clemson Spineless' okra is an extremely easy crop to grow from seed sown directly in the garden when the soil is warm. Sow seeds about ½ to 1 inch deep and about 3 inches apart in rows 3 feet apart. Thin the seedlings to stand 2 to 3 feet apart. Mulch them to conserve moisture and keep weeds down. Using a sharp knife, harvest when the huge green pods turn brown with beige striations. Save some of the seeds for next year's crop before using the pods in your craft projects.

Osage orange (*Maclura pomifera*), also known as hedge apple, is a native American tree. The large thorns and dense branching structure made it an excellent tree for settlers to plant on their property lines to keep cattle from straying. Generations of children have enjoyed playing with the knobby green fruits. Osage orange fruits drop in the autumn and are quite decorative. You can slice and dry them (see "Fabulous Dried Fruits" on page 26 for complete drying instructions) or use them whole in decorations. Their wrinkled chartreuse skins look wonderful in a basket or pewter bowl combined with whole pomegranates and sprigs of holly or other fresh greens.

Drying

Before setting the pomegranates to dry, try inserting a 4-inch floral pick inside each, almost through the blossom end. As the fruit dries it will shrink around the pick, holding it firm. When ready to decorate, instead of gluing the fruit to the wreath, stick the pick down through the greens. Secure to the back of the wreath frame with wire, if needed.

For details on drying other fruits, see "Fabulous Dried Fruits" on page 26. Dried materials are lighter and last much longer than fresh fruit.

Flowering Kale Centerpiece

Flowering kales are really not flowers at all, but attractively colored leaves that have a highly decorative effect. When cut, flowering kale makes an unusual fresh centerpiece. Kale is not a long-lasting plant once cut and brought indoors. Plan on making your arrangement not more than one day ahead of when wanted, and count on a five-day life span.

WHAT YOU NEED

1 to 4 heads of fresh-cut flowering kale, with long
    stems
Interesting basket (lined with a plastic bowl) or
    ceramic container

WHAT YOU DO

1. Rinse the heads of kale carefully to remove any soil clinging to the plant.

2. Add water to the plastic bowl or ceramic container and nestle the kale so it rises above the basket or container rim.

3. To minimize the slight aroma, keep the kale in water and mist daily.

Variation: On a covered porch or stoop by your front or side door, place several heads of kale in a red lacquered basket. To add height to the arrangement, you can wedge a block of saturated green floral foam into the plastic liner, and insert the kale stem into the foam. (To saturate the foam, soak it in a bucket of water for 20 to 30 minutes.) Add cones of bright-red sumac berries and some twigs, bark, or dried shelf fungus. The basket will look like a winter harvest still life.

PROJECT POINTERS

Growing

Kale is one of the easiest plants to grow. It has no pest or disease problems when planted in a loose, sandy soil. I first got hooked on flowering kale after receiving a free pack of seeds from a source long forgotten. I planted them begrudgingly and only because I find it hard to waste seed. It was just a boring little green head for most of the year and I almost yanked it out. It wasn't until after a light early frost that my kale started to look interesting. I dug up four from the cutting garden and replanted them in large terra-cotta pots by the path leading to a barn door. There they kept company with potted mums and were admired by visitors. Long after the mums had gone by, the kale still looked prime. A woman told me that they're also called Christmas cabbages since they last here at least until Christmas.

Cover the long, leafless stems of potted kales by sticking cuttings of boxwood, Japanese holly, or other greens with their stem ends in the soil mix to get some moisture.

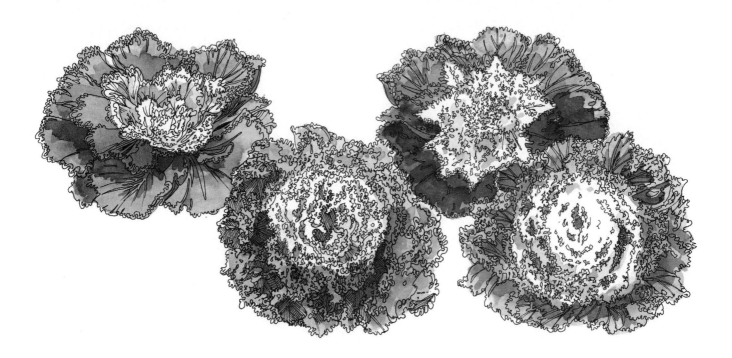

Winter Mantelpiece

For a change from a standard floral arrangement, try this unusual Winter Mantelpiece. This type of composition, called a parallel design, is most effective when you pay attention to placing most of the material upright in the floral foam. You may even have to trim off some side branches that interfere with the vertical line. This design is satisfying with contemporary, country, or traditional interiors.

WHAT YOU NEED

Dried plant materials, including wheat, white larkspur, bells-of-Ireland, pinecones, mosses, and shelf/bracket fungus

Fresh-cut plant materials, including Scotch broom, birch bark and twigs, Colorado blue spruce, boxwood, and winterberry

Green sheet moss or Spanish moss

6 bricks of green floral foam, each 9 inches long, or some green floral foam for fresh-cut material and some brown for dried material

Sharp knife

Pruning shears

12 plastic containers, to hold a half brick of foam each

Hot glue gun and glue sticks, or floral clay

3 tapers, 15 inches tall

2 tapers, 9 inches tall

1 pillar candle, 3 to 5 inches tall

5 candle prongs or your own candlesticks

WHAT YOU DO

1. Cut the bricks of floral foam in half. If using green floral foam, saturate six of the cut pieces in water (do not soak brown foam, if you are using it). Place each piece of foam in a plastic container.

2. Make a plan. Think of trees and plants growing in a wood; think of vertical lines. Tapered candles repeat the vertical lines. Also think of grouping similar materials, and repeating some of those groups at different heights.

3. Line up the foam-filled containers toward the back of the mantelpiece. Some of them should be moved slightly forward to increase the look of depth. Fresh material goes in the saturated foam, dry material in the dry foam. Insert the candle prongs into either type of foam where desired, and add the tapers.

4. The short materials, such as mosses and cones, fill in the front of the composition and hide the containers. Some additional short greens will do that, too. If necessary, glue or secure them to the containers with glue or floral clay. Add the short pillar candle. Never leave a lit candle unattended.

Variations: Decorating a mantel has become traditional for Christmas but not for the rest of the year. Using these same instructions, you can easily create a lovely mantelpiece arrangement for an important occasion in any season. Your guests will enjoy it all the more for its originality.

For an early spring party, for example, you can choose a color theme of yellow and peach. Replace the stark-looking wheat with dried yarrow or *Helipterum humboldtianum*. Use stems of forsythia instead of winterberry, and add some early peach and yellow tulips to the brick of green floral foam. Replace the blue candles with peach or yellow ones. The remaining greens like broom and boxwood will still look appropriate, since they'll be sporting their new spring growth in yellowish or bluish green.

For a summer mantelpiece decoration, you can alter the color theme again and change the whole look of the arrangement. A multi-colored theme can make your mantel look like a colorful perennial border. For the tallest elements, choose stems of fresh blue or purple delphinium or larkspur, which will dry in place in their green floral foam base. Fresh bells-of-Ireland will do the same; they dry to a lovely soft green as the water in the green foam evaporates. Add red, peach, or pink sage for a cheery note. Use the greens listed, or switch to something different like variegated Japanese pieris or a yellow-tinged false cypress. Replace the dried wheat with any fresh wild or cultivated green grass like green foxtail. Choose candle colors to highlight one of the flowers.

For a fall mantelpiece, many materials spring readily to mind. Instead of the winterberry and all of the conifer greens, choose among the wide range of dried grains and grasses. Add dried decorative corn, small gourds, and squash instead of the cones. Candles in a deep-golden shade will complete the theme.

Ornament Mosaics

If you want a new theme for decorating your Christmas tree, look no further than your garden. Dried flowers are dramatic against the dark evergreen foliage. Try these Ornament Mosaics, which combine dried flowers with the gleam of traditional glass balls. Create the mosaics with some of your smallest flowers, or cut large flowers like cockscomb into smaller pieces to get the appropriate size.

WHAT YOU NEED (for one ornament)

Assortment of small flowers, petals, berries, leaves, and cones, including foxtails, globe amaranths, *Helipterum humboldtianum*, pearly everlastings, strawflowers, tansies, and winged everlastings
Cup
Cotton or moss
1 plain glass ball of any color
Thick white craft glue or hot glue gun and glue sticks
About 1 foot of narrow ribbon (optional)

WHAT YOU DO

1. Choose a cup that can hold the glass ball securely while leaving the top half exposed. Line it with the cotton or moss. The soft lining protects the fragile glass while you decorate it.

2. Decide on a pattern for the ornament decoration, using the plant materials you have available. A pattern that is regular and repetitive looks best. Start gluing from the top of the ball down the sides, turning the ball to work evenly around the circumference.

3. If desired, tie the narrow ribbon in a bow around the neck of the ball to finish off the decoration. Let the ribbon tails hang down about 2 inches below the bottom of the ball.

PROJECT POINTERS

Design

Each year, volunteers at the Winterthur Museum of Decorative Arts near Wilmington, Delaware, trim a huge Christmas tree in the conservatory. They use dried flowers as the only trim, and the results are spectacular. You can use the ornament mosaics shown here along with other dried flowers to create a delightful and natural-looking tree.

To decorate the tree, start with stems of rose-tinged hydrangea nestled among the branches. The mass of the flower heads will hold them in place; no wiring is needed. Accent the tree with other large-headed flowers like velvety pink or burgundy cockscomb. Add stems of dried baby's-breath all over the tree to replace tinsel or garland. Group smaller materials into bouquets, wrap the stems with wire, and use the end of the wire to attach the bundles to the tree.

Herbs and other materials are also ideal for decorating a tree. Although dried scented geranium and lemon verbena leaves are not particularly attractive, bunches tucked between the tree branches will emit a delightful scent as the warm room air circulates around them.

Winter Pond

If you want a special design that will last well after the holidays, try this Winter Pond project, with a range of natural materials in reds, whites, and silvers. For extra interest, add a few candles in the center of the "pond," where their glow will be reflected in the mirror.

WHAT YOU NEED

2 or 3 bunches of dried German statice

Assortment of dried plant materials, including poppy pods, gray moss, red cockscomb, red plumed celosia, red-twig dogwood branches, pussy willow, and red sumac berry clusters

Several kinds of conifer cones

Flat white paint (optional)

Small paintbrush (optional)

Fresh-cut greens (optional)

18-inch-diameter mirror, with attached foam ring, or 18-inch-diameter round mirror, with green floral foam wreath set on top

Hot glue gun and glue sticks

Pruning shears

WHAT YOU DO

1. Cut the German statice into 3-inch-long pieces. Starting on the outside of the wreath, stick the stems into the foam, completely covering the surface with the statice. Now work up to the top of the wreath, making sure that all the flowers look as if they're growing upward. Then continue around the wreath surface, covering as much as possible.

2. Glue the gray moss to the inside base of the wreath where the mirror and the foam meet.

3. If desired, use the paintbrush and white paint to highlight the conifer cones as shown in the photo on the opposite page. Let dry.

4. Add the remaining dried materials (including the cones) in clumps around the ring by sticking the stems into the foam. Hot-glue in the conifer cones for extra security. To get the feeling of a natural setting, all of the dried material except the statice should be pointing upward, as it would grow. Clumping the materials together also mimics the natural growth pattern of the plants.

5. Clean off the mirror. If desired, tuck the fresh greens around the base to add extra color to the display.

PROJECT POINTERS

Harvesting

There are three kinds of sumac growing wild in my area. The only poisonous one, poison sumac (*Rhus vernix*), has white berries. Do not touch or pick this species. Staghorn sumac (*R. typhina*) has velvety mauve seed heads and adds an unusual color and texture to fall flower arrangements. For winter designs, I prefer smooth sumac (*R. glabra*), which has the truest red color.

❧ Late-Winter Swag

I often wait until late winter to do some light pruning on my trees and shrubs, when they are bare and their structure is evident. These trimmings are perfect for a variety of projects, such as this Late-Winter Swag. The swollen leaf or flower buds add an important textural note to the "bare" branches.

WHAT YOU NEED

**About 16 branches of birch or other tree or
shrub prunings, 24 to 30 inches long**
**Assortment of cockscomb, lamb's-ears, straw-
flowers, German statice, pepperberries,
and other flowers**
Floral spool wire
4-inch floral picks
Floral wrapping tape
**Hot glue gun and glue sticks, or thick white
craft glue**
2 yards of decorative ribbon
6 inches of thin wire

WHAT YOU DO

1. Divide the branches into two piles of about
eight branches each. Place the piles end to end,
overlapping them 6 inches.

2. Bind securely with the floral spool wire.
Leave some extra wire and make a loop in the
center for hanging.

3. Add stems of cockscomb, about 1 foot
long. (If the stems aren't long enough, extend
them with the floral picks and tape.) Keep the two
sides of the swag evenly balanced. Insert some
stems of cockscomb from each direction, pushing
their stem ends firmly into the pack of branches
so they are held under the wrapped wire.

4. Make a bow with the ribbon and the thin
wire. See Appendix A on page 144 for complete
instructions. Use floral spool wire or glue to attach
the bow to the center of the swag, allowing the
tails to float out along the branches.

5. Now add the other flowers and the pepperberries, trying to keep the materials on the
two sides evenly balanced. Whenever you are
designing, think of the final placement of the
piece. Although most of the construction will
take place while the materials are lying flat on a
work table, you may be looking at the completed
piece from a very different vantage point, perhaps while it hangs high over a window or door.
The bare spots and focal points will appear very
different when you are looking directly down on
the swag versus when you are looking at them 3
feet above eye level on a wall. Keep checking your
design by holding it up to the approximate final

height, and pay particular attention to the bottom and sides.

6. Hang the finished project on a wall, over a
doorway, over a mirror or picture, or in another
suitable place.

Step 3

🌱 PROJECT POINTERS

Harvesting

Pruning chores left undone throughout
the year can often be accomplished in late
winter, when there's little else to do in the
garden. You will almost certainly lose some
spring bloom, but the advantage of seeing
the plant's "skeleton" as you prune can
compensate.

✌ Christmas Wreath

For something a little different, try making a Christmas Wreath of nontraditional materials in red, green, white, and gold. The culinary herbs like garlic, peppers, and rose hips combine with the dried flowers of cockscomb, winged everlasting, and globe centaurea to make a wreath that you can enjoy long after the holiday is over. The dark-green leaves of dried goldenrod provide a needed color accent.

WHAT YOU NEED

21 heads of garlic

21 hot peppers

5 small bunches of goldenrod, picked in the
green stage

15 globe centaurea heads

21 hemlock cones

10 red cockscomb heads

5 sprigs of winged everlasting

21 sprigs of wild rose hips

8 inches of floral spool wire

Floral wrapping tape (optional)

Straw wreath base, 14 inches in diameter

Hot glue gun and glue sticks

WHAT YOU DO

1. Using the wire and tape, if desired, make a wire hanger and attach it to the back of the wreath base. See Appendix B on page 146 for instructions on making and attaching wire hangers.

2. Put the wreath base flat on the table and glue on each garlic head, touching its neighbor, to form a ring. Use plenty of glue on the bottom of each because the garlic is heavy.

3. Next glue on the hot peppers at their stem end, inserting the stems between the heads of garlic. If your peppers are curved at the tips, try to get them all swirling in the same direction.

4. Glue on the rest of the materials one kind at a time, distributing them as evenly as possible. It's easiest to work with the largest materials first, then the smaller. The rose hip sprigs go on last.

PROJECT POINTERS

Growing

While it looks much like a golden thistle, globe centaurea (*Centaurea macrocephala*) is actually more closely related to bachelor's-button (*Centaurea cyanus*). The scaly calyx under the petals of globe centaurea looks very similar to the miniature one on the bachelor's button. Globe centaurea is very easy to grow from seed and will bloom the first year from seed started indoors. The plant will grow to about 3 feet high and 3 feet wide. It will sometimes reseed if you allow some of the flower heads to stay on the plant and set seed. In my garden it has no pests or problems, and I haven't divided it in the six years since planting.

Harvesting

Green is a difficult color to keep in dried material, but you often need it to complete a color scheme. If you pick goldenrod when in bud, before any gold blossoms show, you have a plentiful source of dried greens.

Pick globe centaurea just after the bud begins to open. Flowers will shatter if picked fully opened.

Wild rose hips change color as the season progresses, from green to coral to red after a frost. Pick as they reach the color you want for your project. You can use them fresh and let them dry on the wreath.

Bird's Nest and Potpourri Ornaments

Tree ornaments decorated with natural materials look especially wonderful on your Christmas tree. Small pieces of dried flowers, such as baby's-breath, pearly everlasting, rosebuds, and globe amaranth, and pinecones accent the Bird's Nest Ornament. The Potpourri Ornament is an excellent way to preserve dried petals from a special flower bouquet or corsage.

Bird's Nest Ornament

WHAT YOU NEED

Clump of Spanish moss
2 catalpa pods or twigs, each 10 inches long
Assorted pieces of flowers and berries
1½ feet of 26-gauge floral spool wire
Spray adhesive
Small bird (feathered, painted, or carved)
Hot glue gun and glue sticks, or thick white craft glue
Short piece of ribbon or wire, for hanging (optional)

WHAT YOU DO

1. Take the clump of Spanish moss and gently pull it out to make a long connected string about 1 yard long. If it breaks, it will re-adhere when you squeeze it together.

2. Wrap the string of moss around the wire in spiral fashion.

3. Coil the wrapped wire into a nest shape and, with your hands, continue to shape and pat as if you were working a piece of clay. Hollow out the inside of the nest.

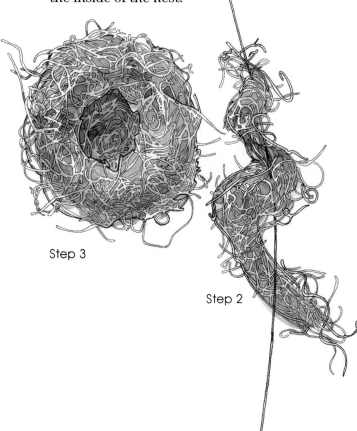

Step 3

Step 2

4. Spray the formed nest with two coats of adhesive. Before it is completely dry, shape and pat the nest again to help it hold its shape.

5. Poke the catalpa pods or twigs through the bottom of the nest in crisscross fashion.

6. Position the bird in the nest and glue it in place.

7. Add dried flowers and berries in a pleasing arrangement. Flowers can reach above or around the bird to give the effect of a hidden bower. Glue each in place.

8. Tuck the ornament between the boughs of a Christmas tree. If desired, add a ribbon or wire for hanging. The nest will also sit nicely on a table or shelf.

Potpourri Ornament

WHAT YOU NEED

Bright petals or small flower pieces
Glass ornament with removeable top
Funnel
Small stick, to use as a pusher

WHAT YOU DO

1. Remove the metal top from the ornament. Using the funnel and the stick, place the petals or flower pieces in the ornament. Gently press them in, until the ball is two-thirds full.

2. Replace the metal top and hang the ornament.

Pressed-Flower Note Cards and Frames

If you're looking for distinctive gifts, these cards and frames never fail to give pleasure. Decorate the Pressed-Flower Note Cards (*foreground*) solely with plant materials, or add papers and strings as well. Cherished invitations, photos, announcements, clippings, and diplomas look impressive in a Pressed-Flower Frame (*background*).

Pressed-Flower Note Cards

WHAT YOU NEED

Assortment of pressed flowers, petals, and
leaves
Blank note cards and envelopes, of fine-quality
paper or card stock
Small pieces of decorative paper or foil
(optional)
Lace or embroidery floss (optional)
Bits of metallic thread or pieces of ribbon
(optional)
Toothpick
Thick white craft glue
Piece of raffia (optional)
Scissors
Small plastic sandwich bag

WHAT YOU DO

1. Plan the design to coordinate with the
card color you have selected. Each card will use
about five pieces of plant material in addition to
the other collage material.

2. If using the decorative paper or foil, tear
it, leaving irregular edges, or cut it into geometric
shapes with sharp scissors. If using lace or embroidery floss, cut to desired size.

3. Using the toothpick to apply the glue, dot
the edges of the paper or foil and lace or embroidery floss with glue and press down on the card.

4. Add the flowers and leaves as desired, putting tiny dots of glue around the edges of each piece
before pressing them down on the card. If desired,
add any bits of thread or ribbon at this point.

5. Let the cards set out to dry for a few
hours. If desired, bundle them together with their
envelopes and tie with a raffia bow. Although it's
best to store these cards in a plastic bag to keep
out humidity, I don't cover the individual cards
with plastic or other material because people
love to touch and smell the real flowers. And
there's no need to worry about sending the cards
through the mail—they travel without damage.

Pressed-Flower Frames

WHAT YOU NEED

Assortment of small pressed flowers, petals,
buds, and leaves
Thick white craft glue
Toothpick
Tweezers
Small scissors
2 acid-free or museum board mats of equal size,
slightly larger than the item to be matted

WHAT YOU DO

1. Ask your framer to cut an opening in the
center of one of the mats to fit your item, leaving
at least a 1½-inch border. The opening should be
a little smaller than the item that is going to be
matted. Leave the other mat whole; it will go
behind the item.

2. Decide on your design. Usually only part
of the mat is decorated—the four corners, an L
shape with two sides connected, a U shape on
three sides, or a large medallion at the top and
bottom. When you plan your flower design, leave
at least ¼ inch from the outer edge because the
frame will cover up part of the mat.

3. If you have the item to be framed, glue
that to the bottom mat, measuring carefully to
place it in the center of the space. If you are
giving the flowered mat by itself as a gift, you will
be working with a blank center.

4. Glue your flowers to the mat using dots of
glue in strategic locations. Using the toothpick to
apply the glue, dot the plant materials with the
glue and press down on the card. The leaves go
on first, forming the outside edges of the border.
Next glue on the small buds and petals, then fine
material like baby's-breath, then the larger flowers.
End by filling in where you feel it looks too bare.
Whether you have used a colored or a white mat,
remember that the spaces that show between
the flowers are part of the design.

5. The finished project should be left overnight for the glue to dry, then stored in a plastic
bag until you can frame it under glass. When
framed, the glass pressing against the flowers
will help to hold them flat.

Artemisia Diamond

When is a wreath not a wreath? When it can hang on the wall or door but isn't round. The Artemisia Diamond is a change from the ubiquitous circle for a wall hanging, a Christmas design that looks appropriate throughout the winter and beyond. The diamond shape is sleek and trim. Turned, it becomes a square. The 'Silver King' artemisia emits a pungent fragrance as you brush by it in your home.

WHAT YOU NEED

24 stems of 'Silver King' artemisia, about 2 feet long
8 white strawflowers
16 red roses and their leaves
16 white helipterums
8 strands of raffia
Hot glue gun and glue sticks, or thick white craft glue
Pruning shears

WHAT YOU DO

1. Divide the artemisia into eight piles of three stems each. Keep the tips of the flower ends even. In order to achieve the straight line effect, you may have to trim the side-branching stems of the artemisia. If your stems are too full, it will detract from the sleek quality of the design. This is one place where more isn't better.

2. Take two piles and lay them end to end. The ends of one pile should lie under the flowers of the opposite pile, making a new grouping 32 inches long.

3. Repeat this process three more times with the rest of the artemisia. You will now have the four bundles for the design lying on your work table.

Step 6

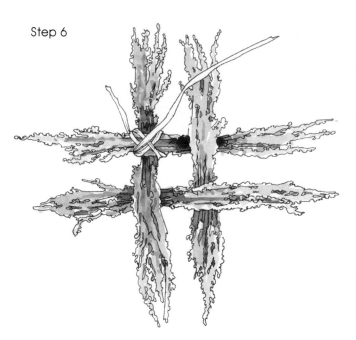

4. Cut four of the strands of raffia in half. Bind the artemisia stems together at a point 13 inches in from the flower tips at each end of the bundle. As you work, try to hide the stem ends under the flower tips. Repeat until all of the stems are securely tied. Trim off the excess raffia so it doesn't show in the finished design.

5. To form the final shape, make a tic-tac-toe design with the four bundles. The center should form an 8 × 8-inch square. The piece will look best if you interweave the bundles in an under-over design.

6. Bind each of the four intersections of the bundles with a strand of raffia. To get a secure joint, cross over the intersection several times and tie it in the back.

7. After all this hard work, you're ready to decorate. Glue a white strawflower in the center of each intersection. Glue on four roses with their leaves in a square around each strawflower. Glue four helipterums between the roses at each intersection. Finish with a second white strawflower on top of each of the first ones for added depth.

8. Trim off any excess stems or raffia, and your diamond is ready to hang.

Variation: As with many of the wall pieces I make, this design also looks interesting as a table centerpiece. Shorten the stems of the artemisia to 20 inches and the overall length of each completed bundle to 26 inches. Place the finished design on a white linen cloth with frosted glass votive candle holders in its center. Always keep an eye on the flames of candles that are near dried materials.

PROJECT POINTERS

Harvesting

Pick the artemisia when it's in bud, before the tiny yellow flowers open, to keep the icy silver color most desirable for this project. Likewise, pick the white strawflowers before they open, to avoid a dark center. Roses should be picked in the half-open stage. They shrink by about one-third when dry.

Drying

Air dry roses by hanging them upside down in a warm, dark spot.

Treasure Gift Wrap

Don't discard those faded or discolored dried flowers! Recycle them into a keepsake gift wrap that is appropriate for the holidays or for a wedding, an anniversary, or any special occasion. Spraying flowers with gold or silver paint can highlight the natural structure of the flower and make fragile petals sturdier.

WHAT YOU NEED

Assortment of faded dried flowers, especially those with interesting structure
Brick of brown floral foam
Gold or silver spray paint
Recycled box with lid
Gold, silver, or white gift wrap
Scissors
Double-sided tape
Gold or silver ribbons of different widths
Hot glue gun and glue sticks, or thick white craft glue

WHAT YOU DO

1. Before working with flowers that may have been lying around for years, gently blow off some of the dust. Stand flowers individually in the floral foam and spray them with the gold or silver paint. Cover each flower completely. It may take several coats. Let dry.

2. Wrap the bottom and lid of the box separately. First, lay the paper on the table good-side down. Put the bottom of the box on the paper and measure how much you'll need to go up the sides and inside about 2 inches. Cut the paper to size.

3. Now wrap the bottom as evenly as you can, using the tape to make the inside look neat.

4. Take a wide ribbon. Measure a piece long enough to go from inside the box, around the bottom of the box, and up into the inside of the opposite side of the box. Center the ribbon and tape it in place. Measure a second piece of ribbon long enough to go around the bottom of the box in the same manner, crisscrossing the first ribbon. Center the ribbon and tape it in place.

5. Repeat Steps 2 through 4 with the box lid. Be sure that the ribbons on the lid are also centered before taping, so they will match up with the ribbons on the bottom when the package is complete. Place the wrapped lid on the wrapped bottom.

6. Make a full bow of the wide ribbon and glue in place where the ribbons cross on the box lid. Add any other small bows or streamers of narrow ribbon in the same color. Glue in place.

7. Position the gilded flowers so they will be highly visible, and glue them in place.

PROJECT POINTERS

Construction

Treasure gift wrap is a great way to reuse old or damaged dried flowers. Once you start looking, you'll find lots of candidates for this project. Recycle the faded blooms from a favorite dried arrangement or from the deep-red Valentine's Day roses that turned from red to black during the drying process. Maybe you waited too long to pick the hydrangea, and the wonderful wine shade has turned to beige or the strawflowers opened too much and the centers have turned an unattractive gray. All of these "failures" can be revived with a touch of spray paint.

Each plant material will take paint in a different way, depending on the surface texture. Smooth pods like okra and smooth-petaled flowers like hydrangea will glisten. Flowers with a fuzzy texture, like goldenrod, will appear much more dull. When you paint a variety of flowers in one color, you will notice not only the shapes and textures but also the differences in color tone.

There is no need to invest in fancy paint for this project. I found the best and cheapest at my local hardware store for under $3 per large can. The gold and silver are bright and clear. For variety, try the copper paint, which contrasts well with almost any color.

You can accent any gift wrap with dried flowers that you have gilded. The key to this project is to wrap the top and bottom of the box separately before you decorate it. The box itself then becomes a treasured gift that can be reused after the present inside is put away.

Kissing Ball and Window Trim

Start a new Christmas tradition in your home with a Kissing Ball (*top*) and boxwood Window Trim (*background*). I first saw this Window Trim at the Winterthur Museum in Delaware, in a Colonial room decorated for Christmas with greens and fruits. In my own adaptation, a hot glue gun provides a practical but unauthentic method of attachment. The Kissing Ball is fun for children and adults to work on together.

Kissing Ball

WHAT YOU NEED

Assortment of dried flowers
1 helium-quality round or oval latex balloon
1-foot-long piece of string
4 yards of paper ribbon
Old newspapers
2 cups of undiluted liquid starch
Bowl, for starch
4 yards of thin decorative ribbon
Tweezers (optional)
Hot glue gun and glue sticks, or thick white craft
    glue
Wide-mouth glass or old coffee can
Scissors

WHAT YOU DO

1. Blow up the balloon to about 1 foot long and tie with a knot. Tie the string on the knot.

2. Cut the paper ribbon into six 2-foot lengths. Cut each length into eight pieces the long way. You'll have 48 skinny strips of paper ribbon.

3. Cover your table with old newspaper. Pour the starch in the bowl, put in half of the paper ribbon, and let soak for 5 minutes. As you need more strips, soak more. (Note: The starch washes easily from hands, clothing, and tables. However, don't get this project wet after completion, because starch also washes easily from carefully constructed kissing balls.)

4. Take one strip of paper ribbon and gently squeeze out most of the excess starch. Start with the string end and wrap the balloon vertically. Give the balloon a quarter turn and wrap vertically again. Continue to wrap, changing directions. Smooth out any humps as you go. When one ribbon ends, start with another. The object is to crisscross strands in many different places and as evenly as possible so there are no large gaps in the wrapping. You do want to leave some spaces, however, since this kissing ball will have an open, airy look when finished. Depending on how far you have inflated the balloon, you may not need all of the strips.

5. Hang the balloon to dry, not touching anything, and with old newspaper underneath to catch excess drips. I hang mine on a shower curtain rod in a guest bathroom.

6. Wait for the paper ribbon to dry completely, about two days. Check the bottom carefully for moisture. When dry, pop the balloon and you should have a beautiful, stiff globe to work with.

7. Remove the pieces of broken balloon from inside the globe; you may want to use a pair of tweezers for this. Fish about 1 yard of decorative ribbon through the balloon-string end of the globe to make a new hanger.

8. Now you can decorate the top and bottom of the globe, using the glass or can to set it on while you work. Check to see that the "south pole" matches up directly under the "north pole" and that the "world" is not askew before you glue

Step 4

on the bottom decorations. Keep the decorations light and simple so you don't put too much strain on the globe. Using 1 yard of the decorative ribbon, tie a perky, simple bow and glue it to the top of the globe. Using the remaining decorative ribbon, tie a more elaborate bow, and glue it to the bottom of the globe. Glue dried flowers to the bows until you are pleased with the result.

Variation: A kissing ball can also be a wonderful decoration for a bridal shower. Follow the same directions above, but change the color of the paper ribbon to match the color scheme of the party, or make it all white with white flowers. Hang the finished ball from the top woodwork of a doorway or window, or suspend it from the center of a dining room chandelier. The ball becomes part of the centerpiece as it "floats" over the buffet table.

At the end of the season, you'll want to take down the kissing ball to make room for a new project. Pack the ball away in a sturdy box, and reuse it the following year.

PROJECT POINTERS

Construction

When you make any craft or arrangement, keep in mind the vantage point from which it will be viewed. The way you position the flowers will be different depending on the view. Will you be looking down on the project (such as an arrangement for a coffee table) or up at the project (such as this kissing ball)? It is often tricky to get the right balance of materials on something you will be looking up at. While you are constructing the ball, you are working at table height, but when you hang the ball up, the bottom decoration (or lack of it) is much more visible. Sometimes I make a project in place so I can get the placement just right, but this is nearly impossible with this kissing ball. If you don't have an area where you can hang the ball up as you work on it, make sure you keep checking the bottom decoration by holding the ball up as high as you can reach to get a bottom view.

Window Trim

WHAT YOU NEED

Sprigs of fresh-cut boxwood, about 5 inches long, 1 for each pane to be decorated
Hot glue gun and glue sticks

WHAT YOU DO

1. If any boxwood sprigs are too dense, trim off the extra leaves.

2. Squeeze a glob of glue onto the back of one sprig and glue it to a windowpane with the end of the sprig positioned at the bottom center of the pane. Occasionally, the hot glue doesn't hold if it gets too frigid, and the boxwood pops off. I just reglue it.

3. When you want to remove the decorations, the glue should pop off easily.

Step 2

PROJECT POINTERS

Growing

Boxwood (*Buxus* spp.) is a slow-growing shrub that enjoys full sun or partial shade. The dwarf cultivars, such as edging boxwood (*Buxus sempervirens* 'Suffruticosa'), are traditionally used in herb gardens as edging plants. Larger species and cultivars can be shrubby or treelike and often reach 8 to 10 feet in height if not pruned. These taller kinds were often planted on estates for hedges or for shearing into fanciful topiary shapes. Many boxwood cultivars are available, some with white- or yellow-variegated or twisted branches. Hardiness varies depending on species and cultivar.

Plant boxwoods in spring in evenly moist, well-drained soil. A site protected from direct sun and wind will keep leaves from turning brown and branch tips from dying back. Boxwoods appreciate a layer of organic mulch to keep the weeds down and to keep the shallow roots cool and moist.

Harvesting

I rarely prune my boxwood but instead let it grow free until I want some for fresh or dried arrangements. If you want to dry the boxwood, pick it in late summer through winter; the tender spring leaf growth tends to shrivel rather than dry and keep its shape. As you pick for your craft projects, keep an eye on the overall shape of the shrub so you trim it evenly as you harvest your crop.

Drying

Boxwood dries slowly, so it should look fresh on your windows for weeks. Even after it is completely dry, the green color remains and the decoration should look acceptable for much of the winter.

When I want to use boxwood in a wreath or arrangement in combination with dried material, I usually start with fresh boxwood and let it dry in place for a more natural look. It bends when fresh and is very brittle when dry.

APPENDIX A

How to Make a Bow

Bows can give even the simplest project a finished look. It's often best to attach a bow to a dried flower project near the beginning of construction and build the flowers around it, rather than in the reverse sequence. Although we often think of the bow as the crowning touch to a project, it takes up a lot of space and requires much handling of the piece to get it attached properly. It's easier to do this before all the fragile dried flowers are in place. Here is how I make a bow using a ribbon that's the same on both sides.

WHAT YOU NEED

2 yards of ribbon
6 inches of thin wire
Scissors

WHAT YOU DO

1. Place the ribbon flat in your palm and hold it under your thumb 11 inches from one end.

Step 1

2. With the longer "tail" of the ribbon, make a loop 4 inches long, and hold it under your thumb.

Step 2

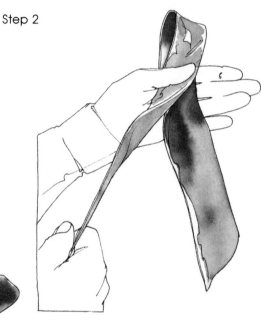

3. Make another 4-inch loop in the opposite direction, and secure it with your thumb.

Step 3

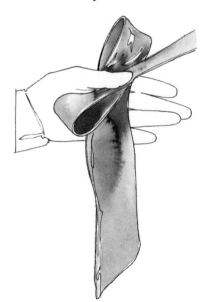

4. Continue forming additional pairs of loops to the left and right, each time making the pairs about ½ inch smaller. You will have enough ribbon to make two to four pairs of loops, depending on the width of the ribbon and the proportions you want.

5. Still holding the bow under your thumb, make one small loop of ribbon in the center, about 1 inch in diameter. Let the tail come down behind this small loop.

Step 5

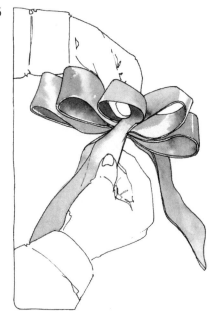

6. Put the wire through the center of the small loop and pull tightly behind the bow. Twist the wire to secure all the loops.

Step 6

7. Cut the tails of the ribbon on an angle.

8. Use the extra wire to attach the bow to your project.

APPENDIX B

How to Make a Wreath Hanger

Attach the hanger to the wreath form *before* you decorate the wreath. Otherwise, you might crush some of the delicate decorations when you turn the wreath over to put on the hanger.

WHAT YOU NEED

8 inches of floral spool wire
Floral wrapping tape (optional)

WHAT YOU DO

1. Cover the wire with the tape, if desired.
2. Twist a small circle in the center of the wire, about ¾ inch in diameter. That forms the hanging loop.
3. Wrap each end of the wire several times around the back of the wreath form until you've used all the wire and the loop is secure.

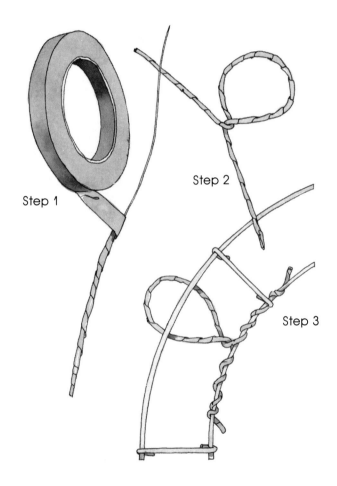

Step 1

Step 2

Step 3

APPENDIX C

Choosing and Using Craft Materials

Having the right materials on hand will help you get the most enjoyment from crafting with your dried flowers. A burst of creative enthusiasm can quickly disappear if you have to hunt around for a suitable wreath frame or drive to the store for a block of floral foam. Fortunately, most of the basic materials are inexpensive and easy to find at your local garden center or craft, hardware, or variety store. Listed below are some of the most common materials you'll need, a brief description of each material and its uses, and sources to give you an idea where you can find each item.

FAVORITE CRAFT MATERIALS

Material	Description/Uses	Sources
Candle prong	Plastic; one end is pointed to insert into floral foam, fruit, or vegetables; the other end supports the candle.	Craft shop, florist or floral supply department

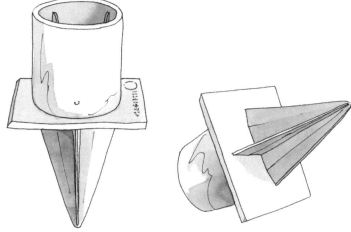

Material	Description/Uses	Sources
Fabric stiffener	Use Aleene's or another brand; follow package directions.	Craft shop, fabric shop
Flame retardant	Spray arranged flowers that will be used around candles to help them resist burning; follow package directions. Never leave treated or untreated plant materials unattended around open flames.	Craft shop, hardware store

(continued)

Material	Description/Uses	Sources
Floral cage	Use instead of a decorative container when the container will be hidden or would interfere with your design. You can buy bricks of green floral foam already encased in a plastic cage.	Craft shop, florist or floral supply department, variety store or five-and-ten
Floral clay	Comes in a roll protected with paper on one side; has the consistency of chewing gum. To use, tear off about 1″, remove the paper and stretch out clay, then press clay on the article you wish to adhere. Make sure the article is completely dry, or the clay won't stick. Works well on glass, plastic, Styrofoam, and baskets.	Florist or floral supply department
Floral foam	For fresh flowers use green bricks, which absorb water. Before using, soak bricks in a bucket of water for 20 to 30 minutes until saturated. For dry flowers use brown bricks, which are non-absorbent. Brown bricks specifically for dried material come in a hard foam, like Styrofoam; use for thick stems and branches. Use softer brown foam for thin, delicate stems. To cut foam, use a sharp paring or steak knife.	Craft shop, florist or floral supply department, variety store or five-and-ten
Floral pick	Use to attach plant material to a wreath, or to lengthen and strengthen stems of dried material in a flower arrangement. Different lengths available. My favorite is a 4″ pick with a 6″ wire attached. You can shorten the pick, if necessary, and cut a new point with pruning shears. To use, take a small bunch of stems and lay the bottom 2″ of stems along the top 2″ of pick. Wrap wire around stems, then secure with a layer of floral wrapping tape.	Florist or floral supply department

Material	Description/Uses	Sources
Floral prong	Use to secure wet or dry foam to a container. Put a layer of floral clay on the bottom of the prong, and press it down into the container. Place floral foam over prong to secure in place.	Craft shop, florist or floral supply department
Floral wrapping tape	Comes in brown, green, white, and other colors. To use, gently pull out a length of tape to stretch it. Wrap stem by overlapping the tape as you twist it around stem. This tape sticks to itself but not to the stem or other things.	Craft shop, florist or floral supply department
Glass dome	Ideal for displaying small dried arrangements, protecting flowers from dust and humidity. Choose the clearest glass you can for best results.	Antique shop, florist or floral supply department, gift shop
Glue, thick white craft	Use for pressed-flower work and many crafts in place of hot glue. It doesn't harden instantly as does hot glue; wait for it to set before continuing with your project.	Craft shop, hardware store, variety store or five-and-ten
Glue gun, cool	Similar to hot glue gun; operates at cooler temperatures. Use for crafts that will be placed outdoors in hot sun or in below-freezing locations.	Craft shop, florist or floral supply department, hardware store

(continued)

149

Material	Description/Uses	Sources
Glue gun, hot	Get a glue gun with self-advancing glue stick. Buy glue sticks that dry clear. Follow package directions. Keep fingers away from dribbling glue. Keep cold water handy for immediately dunking hot fingers into to reduce stinging and prevent blisters. Handy for all craft work.	Craft shop, florist or floral supply department, hardware store, variety store or five-and-ten
Greening pin	Essential for attaching material to a straw wreath base. The most versatile are the 1¾″ pins.	Florist or floral supply department

Material	Description/Uses	Sources
Knife, kitchen	A sharp kitchen knife is handy for trimming or cutting holes in fruits and vegetables. A paring or steak knife is good for cutting floral foam.	Variety store or five-and-ten
Knife, X-acto or utility	X-acto or utility knives are useful when working with pressed flowers or paper projects, such as the Pressed-Flower Note Cards and Frames on page 134. (A razor blade also works well for such projects.)	Craft shop, hardware store

Utility knife

X-acto knife

Material	Description/Uses	Sources
Mirror, with attached foam ring	This product (used in the Winter Pond project on page 126) is manufactured by Knud Neilson.	Craft shop, florist or floral supply department

Material	Description/Uses	Sources
Pinholder	Sharp metal pin; ideal for small arrangements. Secure pinholder to a base with floral clay.	Craft shop, florist or floral supply department
Plaster of paris	Mix according to package directions. Use a disposable container and stick for mixing, as hardened plaster of paris doesn't wash off well.	Craft shop, hardware store
Raffia	A material from the Madagascar palm, used for making bows and knots. It comes dyed in different colors as well as natural. Strands are about 3' long.	Craft shop, variety store or five-and-ten
Ribbon, paper	Comes in rolls, either twisted or untwisted. Buy by the yard or roll. To aid in untwisting, soak the ribbon in water for 5 minutes. Wring out excess water, gently untwist ribbon, and hang over a shower rod to dry. You can also use it straight from the roll as a colored cord in projects.	Craft shop, variety store or five-and-ten
Scissors, household	Useful for cutting ribbon, paper, and thin or soft stems.	Craft shop, hardware store, variety store or five-and-ten
Shears, pruning	Useful for cutting thick or woody stems; wide variety available.	Florist or floral supply department, hardware store

(continued)

Material	Description/Uses	Sources
Silica gel	An excellent desiccant for drying special flowers. Has the appearance and consistency of white sugar. Always use a mask when working with it to prevent breathing the dust.	Craft shop, florist or floral supply department
Spray, protective	True everlastings like straw-flowers need no protective spray. For more delicate flowers and those dried in silica gel, use hair spray or a special floral product like Clear Life spray or Petal Preserve. Spray a light coat over both the front and back of the flower, and repeat when dry. Several light coats are better than one thick layer.	Craft shop, florist or floral supply department, variety store or five-and-ten
Spray adhesive	Helpful when you're working with Spanish moss. A light coat of spray will help the moss hold together and give it a smoother look.	Craft shop, hardware store
Styrofoam	Available in many shapes, including bricks and spheres. Spheres are good for topiaries, like the Dried Topiary Tree project on page 90. Styrofoam is too hard to stick most flower stems into without breaking them; instead, attach your materials with glue or pins.	Craft shop, florist or floral supply department, variety store or five-and-ten
Welting	Cotton stuffing used for the piping that finishes the edges of upholstery. It comes in different widths.	Fabric shop, upholstery shop
Wire, floral spool	Green-coated; comes in different gauges (widths). Higher-number gauges indicate thinner wire. Use 22- or 24-gauge for wrapping material to wreath frames or topiary forms.	Craft shop, florist or floral supply department
Wire, stub	Comes precut in different gauges (widths). Higher-number gauges indicate thinner wire. Buy 16- or 18-gauge for thicker wire, 22- or 24-gauge for thinner wire. "Bright" stub wire looks silvery when new, darkens over time, and rusts when wet; ideal to use for wiring strawflowers and globe amaranth.	Craft shop, florist or floral supply department

Material	Description/Uses	Sources
Wire cutters	Wire cutters are handy for trimming all kinds of floral wire.	Hardware store

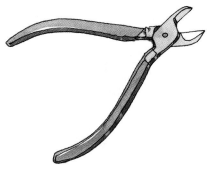

Material	Description/Uses	Sources
Wreath frame	Comes inexpensive and ready-made in different designs and sizes for different purposes. Use a flat wire frame when wrapping dried material to the frame with floral spool wire. Try a deep wire frame when wrapping fresh greens to the frame with floral spool wire. Use greening pins to attach fresh or dried materials to a straw wreath base. Hillman wreath forms come in a variety of shapes and sizes with clasps permanently attached to the forms; you need nothing for attaching fresh or dried materials.	Craft shop, florist or floral supply department, variety store or five-and-ten

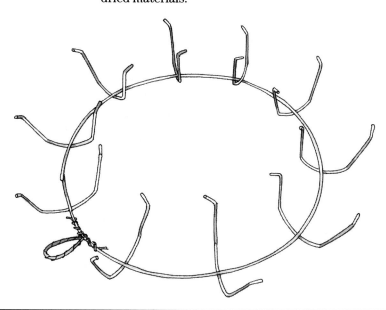

APPENDIX D

Sources

Seeds and Plants

The companies listed below have mail-order catalogs filled with extensive selections of flowers, grasses, and pods to dry. Don't depend on the selection at the local garden center or hardware store. I have noted some of my favorites from each company. Read the fine print in each catalog for other suggestions, and look at the planting information for specific growing hints (such as sun and water requirements and hardiness). As you choose your plants, pay particular attention to their mature height—you don't want to be surprised by short-stemmed blooms when you envisioned a 2-foot-tall flower.

Bountiful Gardens
19550 Walker Rd.
Willits, CA 95490
Sorghum seeds

Harris Seeds
P.O. Box 22960
60 Saginaw Dr.
Rochester, NY 14692
'Turk's Turban', 'Sweet Dumpling', and other decorative squash

Henry Field's Seed & Nursery Co.
P.O. Box 700
415 North Burnett
Shenandoah, IA 51602
Ornamental cotton, many okra cultivars

Johnny's Selected Seeds
2580 Foss Hill Rd.
Albion, ME 04910
'Jack Be Little' pumpkins, 'Burgundy' okra, many everlasting flowers

Nichols Garden Nursery
1190 N. Pacific Highway
Albany, OR 97321
'Turk's Turban' and other ornamental squash, sweet Annie (Artemesia annua) *and other herbs, hops*

Park Seed Co.
P.O. Box 31
Cokesbury Rd.
Greenwood SC 29647
Many everlastings, including Pentzia *'Gold Button', safflower* (Carthamus tinctorius), Craspedia *'Drumstick'; strawflowers separated by color*

Shepherd's Garden Seeds
6116 Highway 9
Felton, CA 95018
Edible flowers and herbs

Thompson & Morgan, Inc.
P.O. Box 1308
Jackson, NJ 08527
Huge variety of flowers and grasses for drying, including hare's-tail grass (Lagurus ovatus), *foxtail* (Setaria spp.), *wheat* (Triticum spp.), *many cultivars of* Helipterum; *strawflowers separated by color*

W. Atlee Burpee & Co.
300 Park Ave.
Warminster, PA 18974
Many Celosia *cultivars, Japanese lanterns, ornamental kale, love-in-a-mist, larkspur, and a wide variety of other flowers for drying*

Wayside Gardens
1 Garden Lane
Hodges, SC 29695
Contorted hazel (Corylus avellana *'Contorta'*)

Materials

Most of the materials used in the crafts in this book are available at your local craft shop, garden center, or hardware or variety store. Appendix C on page 147 lists recommended sources for most of the items you'll need. Here are two sources of specific products.

The Kinsman Co., Inc.
River Rd.
Point Pleasant, PA 18950
Spiral topiary frames

Meadow Lark Flower & Herb Farm
R.D. 1, Box 1568
Orwigsburg, PA 17961
Battenberg lace bobeches, spiral topiary frames

APPENDIX E
Suggested Reading

Here are some useful books on dried flowers and herbs.

Black, Penny. *The Book of Pressed Flowers*. New York: Simon and
Schuster, 1988.
Unusual designs with pressed flowers.

Bradley, Fern Marshall and Barbara W. Ellis, eds. *Rodale's All-New
Encyclopedia of Organic Gardening*. Emmaus, Pa.: Rodale Press,
1992.
Excellent advice on all aspects of growing flowers.

Embertson, Jane. *Pods*. New York: Charles Scribner's Sons, 1979.
*A guide to help you identify plants after flowers and leaves have
gone by.*

Hillier, Malcolm and Colin Hilton. *The Book of Dried Flowers*. New
York: Simon and Schuster, 1986.
A classic book on designing with dried flowers.

Joosten, Titia. *Flower Drying with a Microwave*. Asheville, N.C.: Lark
Books, 1988.
Helpful hints for the often tricky technique of microwave drying.

Kowalchik, Claire, and William H. Hylton, eds. *Rodale's Illustrated
Encyclopedia of Herbs*. Emmaus, Pa.: Rodale Press, 1987.
*A compendium of useful information on culinary and ornamental
herbs and their uses.*

Rogers, Barbara Radcliffe. *The Encyclopedia of Everlastings*. New York:
Wiedenfeld and Nicolson, 1988.
A flower-by-flower description of what to dry and how.

Silber, Mark, and Terry Silber. *The Complete Book of Everlastings*. New
York: Alfred A. Knopf, 1987.
An excellent resource on how to grow specific flowers.

USDA PLANT HARDINESS ZONE MAP

**Average annual
minimum temperature**

Temperature (°F)

Zone 1		Below -50°
Zone 2		-40° to -50°
Zone 3		-30° to -40°
Zone 4		-20° to -30°
Zone 5		-10° to -20°
Zone 6		0° to -10°
Zone 7		10° to 0°
Zone 8		20° to 10°
Zone 9		30° to 20°
Zone 10		40° to 30°

INDEX

Note: Page references in *italic* indicate tables. **Boldface** references indicate illustrations or photos.